THE WORLD ACCORDING TO BESS

A Funny,
Unfiltered Memoir
of Life Lessons from
My 90-Year-Old Mom

Bonnie Lorber Habyan

This work is non-fiction and, as such, reflects the author's memory of the experiences. Many of the names and identifying characteristics of the individuals featured in this book have been changed to protect their privacy, and certain individuals are composites. Dialogue and events have been recreated; in some cases, conversations were edited to convey their substance rather than written exactly as they occurred.

ISBN: 978-1-956955-31-6 (e-book)

ISBN: 978-1-956955-33-0 (paperback)

This book is dedicated to my daughter, Holly, the best accomplishment in my life. May she continue to pave the way by encouraging others to follow their dreams, spreading her own wisdom and ensuring Oreos and ice cream remain a breakfast staple for all grandchildren.

Contents

Author's Note

Generations change like shoe styles and skirt lengths, but values can be passed on to our daughters for eternity. That practice starts now with every parent. Spread your knowledge wisely, deliberately, and when possible, with a sense of humor. That way, it sticks. As Bess says, "I want people to enjoy their lives. It goes too fast. Be good to your children, take care of your families, and get your education, so you don't have to take sh*t from anyone!"

According to Bess, this is the formula for being your Bess-t self.

Introduction

Childhood Memories Are Stickier Than Gorilla Glue

It doesn't matter if you're 10 years old or 90, the things that happen early in life define you and how you see the world.

Whenever I smell Coppertone sunscreen lotion, I think of Ocean City, Maryland—my absolute favorite childhood place. Every time I hear an electric can opener, I think of Jason, the beloved cat I found in my Christmas stocking when I was nine, and when I hear "Silent Night," I think of my mom and all the Christmas Eves I spent next to her in church, hearing our organist play and watching unexplainable tears stream down her cheeks.

As a little girl, this baffled me. Mom rarely cried. *Is she crying because she's happy?* I'd think to myself, grabbing her hand and feeling a little scared.

"I can't help it," she would say every time. "This song always reminds me of my mom because it was her favorite Christmas hymn."

At the time, her answer didn't make much sense to me. My

grandma had died before I was born, so I never met her—and I was probably otherwise preoccupied with the important decision of whether to leave Santa sugar or chocolate chip cookies that night—but I knew even then that I mightily dreaded the day I would have to talk about my own mother in the past tense. Today, my sense of dread has only intensified.

You see, I was blessed to have a mom who loved Christmas and her family above all other things. But lest you think she was a sweet June Cleaver-type of maternal figure, that's not the whole story. She was June on the outside, well-coiffed and buttoned-up, but inside her was a quirkiness Mrs. Cleaver would never have considered, not even in the name of good housekeeping.

Take my memories of fall, for instance. Sure, at my house, there was the aroma of baking apple pie and the cozy smell of wood-fire smoke from the fireplace. But to this day, the arrival of crisp autumn air also brings flashbacks of second-story windows being flung open as family bedclothes were tented out of them like parachutes. Dog-walking neighbors would stare as pillowcases and sheets flapped in the wind, and my mother didn't care. It was her weekly fall ritual to "de-germ" the house. Though I will forever hold dear the scent of holiday sugar cookies, the sweet memories of Christmas gatherings will always be entangled with the shrill sound of my mother screaming, "Run the water when you pee! No one wants to hear that!"

My mom always marched to her own drumbeat, which included a zesty outspokenness that could be a bit sharp and often quite funny, especially to my friends. I remember the time during the '70s gas crisis that I pressed her to take my buddy and me on an excursion. June Cleaver would have calmly explained why it was not feasible, that gas was scarce and prices were through the roof, but my mom responded a tad more robustly with, "Whaddaya want me to do, suck it out of the ground, you nut?" At times, my mother still has that spark and sharpness, but as she ages, her expression has taken new and different forms, along with some colorful sprinklings of swear words.

Bonnie and Bess at ballet recital circa 1969

I should clarify that I did not grow up in a house full of profanity. In fact, on the rare occasions when Mom cursed, it was usually because she was exhausted from a long day's work and the cat had pooped on the rug. But that "f-word," as she still refers to it today, had no place in our home back then. In fact, she categorized anyone she knew who used it as "someone who uses the f-word," adding, "I don't like that f-word. It is uncalled for."

On the very rare occasions a curse word would pop out of my mother's mouth, she would say, "Sh*t—" then pause one second, then another, before saying, "—ger." That was her curse word: Sh*t-ger. According to Mom, a modified curse word didn't count.

As for me, I never cursed growing up. Even as an adult in my early 30s living in Maryland, if anyone heard me utter a curse word, they would say, "That's not like you. Did that just come out of your mouth?" But then, something happened: I moved to Long Island, New York. In the midst of figuring out how to survive in a highly stressful, chaotic environment, I learned that absolutely nothing, and I mean nothing, better relieves stress than the f-word. Sorry, Mom—I love you, but in New York, cursing is sometimes called for.

Bonnie with Santa circa 1971

My 30s are behind me now. Today I am 57 and my mom is 90. At her age, she not only hangs in there; she lets a lot of things hang out now, too. Old age has taken her quirkiness to a whole new level. These days, her filter, which barely existed in the first place, malfunctions a little more frequently. My mom laughs a lot at things others may find inappropriate, and when I get a bit embarrassed, she always responds by rolling her eyes, aggressively waving her hand at me and loudly pooh-poohing, "Oh, that's *nothin'* to say!" Whenever I try to have serious conversations about her questionable remarks, she looks me directly in the eyes and tells me (in various ways), "There's nothing wrong with what I say. You know what your problem is? You take everything so seriously. I used to be like you, but now I don't give a sh*t. Who cares what people think? I'm telling you, you're gonna be dead someday, so have fun now." I don't think June Cleaver ever said that to her kids.

Recently, I had an epiphany about my mother's loosening communication style (which is, unbeknownst to her, a bullhorn through which she emphasizes valuable life lessons). Sometimes, her crazy stories and remarks are like the unintelligible dialogue in a foreign film. Her delivery may be loud and confusing, but when you understand the translation, you realize everything she says is tied to her core beliefs and upbringing, and the higher meaning is revealed—despite the profanities. This "ah-ha" realization has helped my brother and me keep our sh*t together as we struggle to care for a parent we dearly love, even though her resistance to accepting help and insistence on going out of this world her own way often make us throw our arms up in frustration.

Watching your parents age is, well, so many things. The best word to truly describe how this feels is "sucky"—actually, sucky *plus*. As her children, my brother and I have landed in the odd place of taking care of the person who always used to take care of us. My brother is nine years older than I am, and as my only sibling, he still remembers the day I came home from the hospital as a newborn. That day, Miss Fisher, his fourth-grade teacher at Hazelwood Elementary School in Baltimore, allowed him to leave five minutes before the end-of-day dismissal bell rang so he could get a head start on running the mile home to meet me, his baby sister, for the first time as I waited in our mother's arms. My mom says he was surprised at how little I was, but he was happy to have a sibling.

Those were comfortable times, when we both felt loved, safe and protected. But now we find ourselves in a real spot of uncomfortable strain—like we are lost in a maze we can't navigate. Yet on this grueling journey down what I call The Proverbial Rabbit Hole of No Way Out, Mom's covert lessons, camouflaged as bizarre, off-color blurts, are giving us quite a few laughs, head-scratches and "Holy sh*t, she was right!"

moments. We've realized that you can't fight crazy, and that is okay. The older my mother gets, the more I see that the line between sanity and absurdity is, in reality, pretty blurry.

These days, Mom is more than eager to share the vivid details of her childhood. When she does, her insights are often prefaced with, "You should have lived in my day," or "You should have experienced what I did." I understand what she really means is that the increasingly complex world we find ourselves in today is not necessarily better than the one she grew up in. Her stories are a direct invitation for anyone listening to fall back with her, to a time and place where, as seen through her eyes, things were easier and simpler—and as she lets her wisdom loose, those same eyes knowingly glisten at her audience's jaw-dropping disbelief.

My Mom as a Drink: The Bess Margarita

Making a good margarita is easy. The tequila gives the margarita its flair, so the better the tequila, the better the drink. But if you blend two parts party time, an ample pour of zestfulness, a part jigger of Depression-era wisdom, a heaping portion of spicy feistiness, some welcome drops of sweetness and top it all with a sprinkle of sunshine and a spritz of fashion, you don't just get a cocktail, you get Bess.

THE BESS MARGARITA RECIPE
2 ounces blanco tequila (the party time)
1 ounce fresh lime juice (the zestfulness)
½ ounce orange liqueur (the wisdom)
½ ounce agave syrup (the sweetness)
¼ jalapeno pepper (the feistiness)
Garnish with a sugar rim (the sunshine) and a lime wheel (the fashion)

Growing up, I was influenced by all of the ingredients in my mom's personality. In all honesty, I wish I had gotten a bit more of the feistiness and party time. But the real important trait was wisdom. For example, Bess told me many times that I would never understand what it was like to worry until I had my own kids. She was right. You never understand the sheer responsibility and intense love you can have raising another human being until you have a child yourself. But the 1,651 feisty times I heard her say, "Wait until you have your kid, and you'll see," before I had my daughter was like the canned laughter on a sitcom. I heard it—but not really. But she was right.

Now, as she ages, Mom's only advice from this phase of life is simply, "Don't get old." And even though I am not a grandma yet, I know, as we all do, that the "don't get old" advice is hard to heed (physically, at least). When I do become a grandma, I hope my grandkids call me something like "Mémé" or "G-ma" or "Grams." But those names didn't work for Bess! Her maternal nickname needed a shot of something else, something spicier—a tequila floater, if you will. I have twin nephews named Justin and Brandon. When they were babies with bowl cuts, just starting to speak, I began to whisper in their ears, "Don't call her Grandma; call her Bess!" I knew my mom would get a kick out of it, and I would melt watching them do just that, accompanied by snorts and giggles.

As years passed, this tradition not only stuck, it spread. Those now-grown nephews and all the children that followed them—including my niece, Brooke, and my daughter, Holly—call her Bess, too. Some people think it's disrespectful to refer to your mom or grandmom by first name, but quite frankly, who gives a sh*t? For us, it's a true term of endearment. It's our way of celebrating her uniqueness. Besides, Grandma just doesn't seem to be a bold enough name for someone like Bess.

As for that personality of hers, she and I are very different people. But through her eyes, I've learned about what's important in life. And although my inherent Type-A personality may not allow me to embrace every single nugget Bess offers, her drops of wisdom and sprinkles of sunshine frequently make me pause. She recently told me she's had a great life and has no regrets about anything. That's Bess's zest. With the onset of dementia and short-term forgetfulness, she tells me this a lot—at least five times a day. I listen because I've realized that's all any of us wants to be able to say. Bess savors her past and clearly basks in the brilliance of having no regrets.

The truth is most of us, if we're lucky, have had our own Bess: an aunt, a dear friend or a grandma who has given us memorable advice. The perspective my mom offers on being your Bess-t self in the following pages may not be entirely unique, but her way of sharing it certainly is. Whether you have your own Bess or not, I hope you enjoy this refreshing, spirited and spicy blend of her anecdotes, opinions and stories—my mom's lessons for us. Like the Bess Margarita, part salty and part sweet, may this book give you a down-to-earth view of the sh*t that actually matters—and some good belly laughs in the process.

Chapter 1
Lesson One
Growing Up Bess: Do You Have to Feel Poor to Be Poor?

Mom was born Bessie Emma Reese on June 6, 1931 in her home in Baltimore, Maryland at 1521 N. Milton Avenue. As one of four children, she grew up near poverty level, which her younger brother Ken still likes to remind her (and she likes to remind everybody else). At night, they shoveled coal into a furnace to keep themselves warm, used baking soda to brush their teeth, and wrapped their heads in rags soaked in kerosene oil to kill lice. But my mom says she never felt poor. Even as a child, her perspective was positive. I guess that shows what hard work and a well-kept home can do to make children feel safe and comfortable.

Her dad Harry was a streetcar repairman who would wake early to paint houses before going to his full-time job after lunch. Grandpop, or "Pop," as we all called him, was the neighborhood handyman. He often completed jobs as barter for doctor visits or homemade luxuries his family couldn't otherwise afford, like those famous Maryland blue crab cakes. Bess's dad worked six days a week, taking only Wednesdays off. Her mom, Hazel, was a homemaker who died prematurely from cancer at the age of 56, but Pop lived to be 87 and died in 1987. His heart just wore out. Still, 87 is not too bad considering that his diet contained so much scrapple, a regional specialty of pickled pigs feet and canned sardines. Personally, I wouldn't even feed scrapple to a family pet, but things were simpler back then.

Bess really loved her mother. When Grandma Hazel was diagnosed with ovarian cancer, my mom and her younger brother helped take care of her until she died two years later, leaving her without a mom at 22. Bess is convinced her mother went to heaven because before her last breaths, she kept asking her if she could hear the beautiful music and kept telling her how glorious it all looked. Bess's memories of her mom, unlike many of her short-term recollections these days, are vividly clear.

My mom has told me her mother was the quintessential homemaker who would whip up the family dinner at 1 pm in the afternoon so her dad could eat before going to work. She remembers how on Fridays, if her dad had been able to work a little overtime during the week, the family would celebrate with a piece of chocolate bark divided between the four kids. If the week had been slow, they'd get jellied orange slices or enjoy a few crunchy, sugar-coated, green spearmint leaves. "That was a disappointment, but we ate 'em," Bess notes.

Apparently, Grandma Hazel's idea of Sunday leisure time was a two-mile trek from their home in Baltimore to the cemetery to visit her parents' graves. They'd go, rain or shine, after an hour-long church mass. According to Bess, the experience sort of sucked, but she did enjoy the occasional snowstorms that forced them to cancel their tombstone visits. On those days, she and her brothers and sisters would scoop up snow with a cup and pour chocolate milk and Hershey's syrup on top. That was a winter treat, a luxury afforded to all.

Like most families in the Great Depression, Bess's family considered telephones a rich person's luxury. There wasn't one in her house or anyone else's along her street. Whenever someone in the neighborhood had to make an emergency call, they would have to do so at the corner grocery store; likewise, if someone was trying to reach some specific household in the neighborhood, they would call the grocery store (perhaps from another grocery store). After receiving a call, the grocery store owner would have to run to the affected house to deliver the message.

Bess's older brother, who was also named Harry after their dad, was drafted at 18 and served in Korea during World War II, so he often called the store to check in with his parents. Whenever Bess got to carry the message back home that Harry was on the phone, it was like she was presenting her mom with the rarest diamond in the world; the gift she got in return was the glittering joy her message produced.

In those days, girls were groomed to become housekeepers, so when her mother was sick, Bess had to stay home from school to take care of things, do the laundry and make the meals—and she was good at it. It made her feel proud, and I swear it was the origin of her obsession with food. Stepping in to do the cooking for her mom was how she was conditioned to show love to her family and those around her. Bess always enjoyed cooking, and she still frequently reminisces about baking during snowstorms.

"I used to love when it was cold, and the snow would be coming down, and I could bake a cake," she says. "It smelled so good." After asking her about having to stay home for her mom to do laundry and chores, she answers, "Hell, we didn't know anything else. That's what girls were supposed to do." She did it well, excelling in Home Economics, which was required for girls in high school back then. She got an "A" on her dusting ability—imagine that curriculum in today's world!

My mom left high school in the ninth grade and enrolled in Clara Barton Vocational School in Baltimore, Maryland for what was supposed to be a two-year program to become a medical secretary. But when the requirements changed and she was told she would have to spend another year in the program, she said, "Screw that!" and dropped out. Through a friend, she heard about something called keypunching. You could receive a six-week training course in it through IBM and immediately be employable. Bess did well with her training and soon had her first real full-time job at the age of 17, enabling her to pay $10 a week to her parents for room and board. Every day, she and five others from the neighborhood would carpool to work in downtown Baltimore, a steady reaffirmation that she was now independent.

Bess loved being a working girl and being single, but she especially enjoyed the paycheck. She would get it on Fridays, cash it ASAP and run to the nearby women's clothing store called Hecht Company to add to her already extensive wardrobe. She loved to shop, and as she kept working as a keypuncher, her paychecks kept going straight into her attire. Her life as a working girl was a stark contrast to the financial scarcity her family had grown up with, so while she acquired a dashing work wardrobe while still living at home, Bess thought it best to keep it to herself. She hid new clothes from her mom, who would've become upset with her frivolity and might've reported her impractical splurges to her dad (who, in turn, might've raised her rent). At work, however, she earned the title of "New Dress Bess" for her various ensembles.

A few years later, she landed at a new job at American Rolling Mill Company (ARMCO for short) and was nominated for Miss ARMCO, Queen of the Steel Mill, for her congeniality and sense of style. "I think I was first runner-up," she told me when I asked her if she'd won. "I didn't win, but I'm glad the lady who won did. She was our crane operator. She was the only crane operator we had and was with the company forever. I think she got a crown and a $50 US savings bond." Bess said if she had been crowned the Steel Queen, she would have broken the bond way before it matured and invested in a new dress, shoes and purse to match.

Bess dressed in her Bess-T circa 1951

I still remember playing dress-up as a little girl with all of her once-in-vogue, fancy clothes. I especially loved her kolinskies, dead Asian weasels that looked like foxes, and would wrap them elegantly around my neck. Mom told me her Aunt Marie, the alco-holic of the family, wore a

Bess and the Miss ARMCO Queen's Court

kolinsky to a holiday party once, and a mouse jumped out of it. "Christ," Bess said, "everyone screamed and jumped on chairs." To this day, I am not sure if that was one of the same kolinskies I played with, but I do vividly remember its creepy, marble-looking eyes and snout at one end and scaly feet at the other. Sometimes, I would pretend I was going out to a fancy ball;

other times, I would put a kolinsky in my baby doll crib, wrap it in a blanket and feed it a bottle as my baby animal. Just like Mom did with me.

Bess and her friend decked out in kolinskies circa 1952

Chapter 2
Lesson Two

Memories Are Like Jelly Beans— Savor Your Favorites and Leave the Licorice Ones at the Bottom of the Bag

When Bess talks about her childhood, she tells you how good it was. Growing up on a tight budget meant owning one pair of shoes and starting work at an early age. But laughs were free, and so were friendships.

"When my mother would throw us a party," Bess told me, "Christ, she'd invite her friends and all these older people. No kids. I could never understand that. I can't remember all of her friends, but I do remember one. Her name was Margaret McQueer. It never dawned on me that her name was odd until just now. She was always first on the list to be invited. Margaret was from a big family with a lot of kids, but they never came. That was odd. My whole damn family was odd with the birthday party thing. They never invited any of my friends. Just their friends."

Bess and her neighborhood friends raised in Baltimore, MD

Bess was always very social and had a lot of girlfriends growing up, and they found unusual and inexpensive ways to find amusement.

"When I got a little older, around 13, my crazy, loud-mouthed friend Shirley Tarleton and I entertained ourselves in the summer by walking through Baltimore neighborhoods looking for black crepes hanging on the door. That meant someone was dead inside the house. We'd spot a crepe and scream, 'We got one! Let's go in and look!' They'd lay 'em out for three or four days, and the undertaker would come in to fix their faces, patting on pancake makeup that was melting off from the terrible summer humidity. Christ, we did that at least two dozen times. We'd hang out for a while and be really serious and make our way up to the casket to look. Then we'd leave, bust out laughing at the dead guy, and Shirley would mutter something like, 'Christ, he was ugly. Boy, did he have big lips.' That was the highlight of our day." According to Bess, it was the highlight of her summer, too!

"Vacation? Christ, we didn't have any vacation. My mother didn't take us anywhere because the poor soul worked all the time keeping the house together. On my father's day off, we'd go to Carlin's Park, or we'd walk to Clifton Park to get in the public pool. I couldn't swim—lucky I didn't drown. I'd have to rent a black wool bathing suit for a nickel, and it was terrible. Talk about itchy in hundred-degree weather. Christ, that was miserable. But we thought it was great! We didn't have two nickels to rub together."

Bess's short-term memory isn't as sharp as it used to be, but she can recall the deeply embedded memories of her early years quickly. She readily recounts them as teachable moments for the new generations who, according to her, just don't get it. The way Bess lives is heavily influenced by her experience during the Great Depression, even today. So, she can't help but remind us about the way things used to be when doggie daycare was something you'd only see as part of an imaginative Saturday morning cartoon in the 1970s.

On Cat Food

"Cat food? What cat food? Christ, we couldn't afford cat food. Our cat Skinner ate whatever we had left on our plate. We were lucky *we* ate, let alone worry about the damn cat."

On Doctor Visits

"Doctor? You had to be on your death bed to go to the doctor."

On Dentist Visits

"He charged 50 cents for a pulled tooth, and if you got cocaine, he charged you a dollar." Wait, what? Ooh, she meant novocaine!

On Her First Job

"I used to scrub my neighbor's marble steps for 50 cents. These days, kids want to be paid for just looking at the steps."

On Saving Money

"I had a little piggy bank, but it was empty."

Bess says her piggy bank stayed empty her whole childhood. Even so, a few coins rattling around in a ceramic-shaped animal or having the experience of a real vacation were completely immaterial to the fullness of her young life. In fact, Bess freely tells me what she thinks kids are missing out on nowadays. "Kids don't know how to enjoy themselves anymore," she says. "They're stuck in front of those stupid phones. When I was a little girl, we used to play with our doll babies. You never see that anymore. Things have changed. Kids have a lot more money to do different things. We didn't have money. We found ways to entertain ourselves. We used to play a lot of dodgeball and hopscotch, and if we were lucky, my dad would leave us a nickel to go to the movies."

Maybe she's right. How can you compare spending summer days playing virtual reality games to a neighborhood game of hopscotch, or checking out a real, dead, decaying stranger who was ugly and had big lips? Quite frankly, I am not sure if that one is the licorice or cherry jelly bean of life. I venture to say it is all in one's perspective. And by the way, I don't like the black jelly beans, but they are Bess's favorite. She loves the licorice ones.

Chapter 3
Lesson Three
From Sex to Makeup—Listen, Watch and Learn

I asked Bess once who her role model was, and she couldn't answer. As long as I can remember, she had always had friends, but the only person I ever heard her talk about who made a positive impact on her life was her boss at ARMCO, Bill Bishoff.

She has told my brother and me at least 50 times how she is still angry with her father because she thinks he threw away a letter Bill wrote about her in mid-1952. That letter commended her work ethic and her get-it-done attitude. I think she obsesses about it because it was one of the few times, if not the only time, she felt validated for her abilities. That fact is truly sad, if not outright tragic. But despite her lack of recognition, Bess still has a fierce, brave spirit, and it's clear that the situations and people around her have deeply affected her opinions on what it takes to be a good person—especially her mom.

On Her Favorite Christmas Memory

"When I got my Betsy Wetsy doll. It peed when you gave it a bottle."

On Her Favorite Book Ever

"*The Three Little Bears*. I still love that story. It was my favorite book. Come to think about it, it was the only book I ever had, so I guess that's why it was my favorite."

On the Neighborhood Tramps

"We called them bad girls."

On the Birds and Bees

"No one told us nothin'! I remember one day when I was 16, I was grocery shopping with Mom and I said, 'Look, that woman is pregnant!' and she hit me alongside the head. 'Don't say that,' my mom said in a stern whisper. Christ, saying someone was pregnant was like talking about them having sex."

On Her Most Fun Aunt

"Crazy Aunt Marie would come for Sunday dinners and bring a bottle of cheap wine, and she would drink the whole damn thing by herself. We would have to hold her up when she staggered and help her out to the cab at night. After Aunt Marie left, my mother would say, 'Oh, she's a lovely woman.' I couldn't wait 'til Aunt Marie got drunk. We used to cry when she went home because she was so much fun. She smoked like a chimney, one after the other. I can still see her lightin' up a cigarette. Her voice was deep like a man's from all that smokin'."

On Being Nine Months Pregnant and Having No Idea
"One night, my Aunt Gertrude felt sick and went to the hospital and had a baby. Christ, none of us, including her, knew she was pregnant. Can you imagine? How the hell did that happen?"

On Wearing Makeup
"Christ, when my mother saw me wearing makeup, she would tell my older brother Harry, 'Smack her and wipe that lipstick off.' And he would. He loved to do that."

On Her Most Vivid Memory of Her Mom
"I have a lot of those. I remember seeing the scars on her chest and stomach when she would get undressed. They were all white and wrinkly from when she got burned. She told me that when she was around six or seven, she used to wear a little red sweater with holes in it to school. She never had a winter coat. One day, she was standing near a bonfire outside to keep warm on the way to school and got too close. She was burned over her entire stomach. She was in bed for months. Burned right through to her kidneys. She got better, but back then, you didn't stay in school for long."

On Her Mom's Education
"She left school in fourth grade to help at home. She worked herself to death after that. She was a great homemaker. She always had a pot of soup on and a homemade cake for us. She didn't have an education past the third grade, but she knew enough. She was a wonderful woman who loved her family above all else. That's all she had. She'd smack us on the behind

when we needed it, and sometimes, I would get a smack in the face, especially if I was late for dinner. Sometimes, I would run around the table until she caught me. Kids in my neighborhood would get smacked with a yardstick. Nowadays, they don't smack anyone. They sit the kids in time out. I like that."

Chapter 4
Lesson Four
You'll Know When He's the One

In 1949, at age 18, Bess met her Prince Charming—my father Charles Lorber, aka "Buck"—at the beach:

I knew of him around the neighborhood where I lived, but I really got together with him down at the ocean. I was down there on Memorial Day, and I had sun poisoning all over my lips. My sort-of boyfriend George asked me to go to Ocean City with him, and we were supposed to drive down together, but then he told me he couldn't take me because he was taking his friends down, so I had to get a ride with someone else. He took my luggage with him, but I was a little mad. So, I caught a ride with this guy who used to take his ulcer pills with beer.

Anyhow, after we got to Ocean City, I went to bed, and the next day, I woke up and needed my things. So, I walked to meet George where he was staying and this cute man with the most beautiful baby blue eyes ran down the steps and helped me with my luggage. The cute man asked me to meet him at [a bar called] Jackson's at 10 am, so I ran back, put my bathing suit on and went to meet him. We danced all morning and had so much fun. I had agreed to meet George at the big clock at noon. I looked out at the clock and saw George waiting for me, and I thought, 'He didn't care how I got to Ocean City, so screw him.' When we got back to Baltimore, your dad showed up at my house and asked me out again, and we dated on and off for three years until one day, he broke up with me, telling me I wasn't his type.

We had tickets for a dance that weekend, and he said we could still go, but he also said that after the dance was over, he wanted to take out someone else. He showed up at my house that Saturday and I wasn't there. I went out. Screw him, too, I thought. The following Saturday, he went out with the other girl, and afterward, he came to my house and told me he wanted to talk to me. He really looked cute. He told me he missed me, and that we were going to get married in February. Never once during those three years did we even talk about getting married. Once my dad heard we were engaged, he said, 'It's kind of sudden, isn't it?' I thought that was the strangest comment since we had been dating for three years.

Bess and Buck got married on February 22, 1953. She was 22; my dad was 28. My parents had to buy a house near the streetcar line quickly so my grandpop Harry, who was going to live with them, could get to work easily. Three months later, Pop told my mom he was getting remarried and bought a house with his new wife. With the house to themselves, Bess wasn't one to just sit home while Buck was at the office all day. She kept working until my brother Charles Jr., aka "Buddy," was born on September 7, 1956, a few months after my mom's 25th birthday.

Like most women back then, Bess left work and became a full-time mom, enjoying keeping an immaculate home, making sugar cookies around Christmas and eventually learning how to drive. She said she did it for Buddy. "I had to take him to school," she explained. Nine years later, I was born on December 7, 1964. That made us the four B's: Buck, Bess, Bud and Bonnie. I'm not sure if that was on purpose. We lived in a 1,000 square-foot row house in Baltimore until I was 12, when we moved to the "country" a half-hour or so north, to a house in the town of Bel Air, Maryland, where 45 years later, Bess still lives.

My dad truly loved my mother, quirkiness and all. They knew how to have fun together and looked forward to their weekend dances and get-togethers with friends. Dad had a good sense of humor, too, and liked to play occasional jokes on unknowing suspects. I always remember a lot of laughter when we had friends and family visit, a routine that has surely transitioned to my own home celebrations today.

Like her mom, Hazel, Bess always had a freshly baked cake made from scratch for family and visitors. As a little girl, I used to love to help my mom crack the eggs, and I still remember the slight burning smell the mixer's engine made as it cut through the velvety batter. But when I entertain, I prefer to focus on the main course, unlike my mom and grandma. Cakes never stuck as part of my domestic repertoire—too much work and too many calories.

Although I never got the chance to meet Grandma Hazel, I did have the chance to know my grandpop and my step-grand-mom, Pauline. I have very vivid memories of occasionally stopping in with my dad to see Pop at his row house in Baltimore, which always smelled like mothballs. For some reason, Pop often screwed up my name and called me Robin, my cousin. While he and Dad chatted, Pauline would lecture me on the importance of taking care of your teeth so you didn't end up with false ones. She always kept herself nice. She *always* had the most beautifully painted nails, although to me, her hair looked like it was a shade of pale purple, not gray.

Pop had a small front lawn, literally six feet by eight feet, but it was the best-kept lawn in the neighborhood, boasting one of those little "Keep Off Grass" signs you could get from the local hardware store. I liked my visits to Pop's because there were always eastern box turtles in his backyard, which was fenced and also tiny—maybe 10 by 10 feet. He also kept Fresca in his fridge.

As for the turtles, finding them in the grass was sort of like my own game of I Spy. Years later, I found out that my dad had been putting those turtles there a few minutes before our visits as a joke. When he wasn't fooling Pop by unscrewing each of the outside holiday bulbs just enough so he would think the lights were broken, he was collecting a few slowpoke tortoises to get a rise out of his father-in-law.

Dad's work as a Baltimore Gas and Electric Service supervisor had him driving on the local roads a lot, and he often spotted the turtles in the street. He would put them in a box and drop them off in Pop's fenced backyard without telling him. Those turtles in his lawn used to drive Pop crazy. He could never figure out why in the hell he was the only one in the neighborhood who had turtles. But he loved them, and they became his pets for life.

Bess loved her mom but was happy her dad now had a companion, and she was grateful to Pauline for taking such good care of her father. In fact, Pauline shared my mom's philosophy that women should keep themselves attractive for their husbands and look after their men. Thank goodness she had someone to discuss those things with, as some of Bess's comments about women who didn't could be pretty harsh.

"You should see Mrs. Jones. I ran into her at the supermarket and boy has she let herself go. Her hair is completely snow white, no makeup on and she must be 300 pounds. She was dressed in raggedy ol' sweatpants and dirty tenner [sic] shoes. No wonder her husband left her."

Bess always kept herself nice for herself and for my dad. She truly loved him and still does. My dad left high school to join the Marine Corps before marrying my mom. He went back to get his GED at 32 years old before going to night school for business management at Johns Hopkins University in Baltimore. Mom said that one day after dinner, he told her that he wanted to go back to school. "You should go then," she said. "We will figure it out." It took him 12 years to finish his degree. He was so proud of his college ring.

Dad spent his entire working career at Baltimore Gas and Electric. He loved it. For all 45 of his years there, my mom always laid out his work clothes, got up to fix him breakfast every day and made sure he had wonderful, packed lunches. Bess took pride in knowing other men were jealous of my dad's lovingly made ham and cheese sandwiches. Each day, he gave her a kiss on the cheek before he walked out the door and another before they went to bed.

My father, the love of my mother's life, passed away on June 13, 1995, at the age of 70, from prostate cancer. To this day, my mom regrets that she kept his college ring instead of burying him with it, thinking that perhaps my brother or her grandsons would want it someday. Several months later, she was mad at herself. She knew how much that ring meant to him but somehow thought that value could be transferred. She realized after his death that it couldn't be. The ring was his most prized possession, aside from his children, and she would never again have the chance to let Buck take it with him. Bess's life changed forever that day, but the love she still has for him is eternal.

Bess at age 21

Bess and my dad enjoying a boat ride

Their wedding in 1953

Wedding family photo

Chapter 5
Lesson Five
Take Care of Your Hair (but Keep the Vicks Out of Your Nose)

As a child, I felt very clean. That was because my mom was obsessive about germ killing. Our house had a constant stainless-steel glow, sort of like the face of your refrigerator after you use the spray-on cleaner. She even washed down all our walls as part of her twice-a-year cleaning ritual. All this work got harder to do as she aged, and as she approached 85, she somehow talked me into washing her walls for her. The procedure goes like this: you take the car washing bucket, fill it with a cup or two of ammonia, add steaming hot water, throw in an old remnant of a bath towel and wipe away. It turned out to be a two-day project, and the irony was that I don't wash my own f*cking walls!

She kept an immaculate house. It was quite unusual to catch a cold in the Lorber home when I was little, but on the rare occasions that we did, she had her own remedy. In addition to the tear-inducing whiffs of ammonia I would get from her biannual wall baths, I still vividly recall the brain-freezing scent of her favorite cold and sick remedy: Vicks VapoRub.

Vicks was the go-to remedy for my mom because it had been her mom's go-to remedy when she was a child. And I don't just remember smelling this stuff but *feeling* it burning my juvenile nose hairs because, in the Lorber residence, Vicks VapoRub went straight up the schnoz. One day I decided to Google what not to do with Vicks, and bingo, do not ram it up the nostrils was tip number one.

Why did she do that? I wondered. So, I asked.

"So just curious, Mom, why did you put Vicks up my nose when I was little and had a cold?"

"Because that's what people did back then," Bess replied.

"Did your mom do that?" I questioned further.

"Of course. Christ, she would rub it all over our bodies and then put a hot towel on our chests and heat up a little Vicks, put it on a teaspoon with a little sugar and we would eat it. Then, we would have chicken soup."

"Why would she rub it all over your body?"

"What, the chicken soup?"

"No, the Vicks, not the soup. Did you ever ask?"

She looked at me with eyebrows furrowed. "I didn't shove it up your ass. I put it up your nose."

In addition to being clean, I was also very well fed and coiffed. I was so well-coiffed that I'm surprised I didn't end up with permanently puffy hair. From the time I could speak, I accompanied Mom to the hair salon, which was full of middle-aged mothers in a fog of permanent solution and hair spray clouds. The beautician, as they were called back then, would wash Bess's hair, put it in rollers and then put her under one of those old-fashioned drying contraptions, the kind that were chairs with hoods like little umbrellas attached on top. After about a half-hour, the beautician would remove the rollers and tease the sh*t out of the hair, then style it and spray it like you would spray paint a picture frame. This occurred every seven days—religiously.

Bess having a little fun with a good hair day

Bess and I after a day at the beauty shop

When I was eight, I was in the local school's roller-skating show. I wanted to look super sharp, so Bess treated me to a bouffant-deluxe experience: rollers, teasing, hairspray and all. I was the only person in the entire show whose hair was bigger than their skates. I never went back to have my hair done again, but for my mom, hair was the top priority. Bess's unique hairdo and its maintenance outranked everything, including clean walls.

My friends thought my mom's hair affair was pretty funny. When I was a freshman in high school, I waited every day after classes with a friend for my mom to pick me up. And every day, this friend would pray my mother would scratch her head as she approached the pickup area so she could have a good laugh. That's because to do this, Bess had to poke her index finger through all that hair to reach her scalp, gingerly weaving it through the tightly teased locks to prevent any sort of damage. Remember, she had to make her hairdo last for a whole week!

Bess absolutely loved my dad's hair, which was thick his whole life. I have super thick hair too, and to this day, she tells me I got it from my father because hers is so thin. After I graduated college and got married, I had my own beautiful daughter, Holly Elizabeth. Holly had so much hair that when the doctor was trying to figure out how far down the birth canal she was during labor, he warned me she had a head full before she even came out! My mom always says Holly got her good hair from my dad, too. I only wish he had been alive to meet my daughter.

Chapter 6
Lesson Six
Dance Your Ass Off When You Can!

We made a family trip to Ocean City, Maryland every summer in the early 1970s, always leaving in the middle of the night to beat the traffic. My mom would pack the infamous Coppertone sunscreen in our suitcases, placing them and me in the back of our maroon Chevy Impala.

I remember the sound of the crickets chirping and the smell of fresh-cut grass below the morning dew as she laid me on the back seat (no seatbelts back then) with my favorite scratchy blanket, the one my mom's friend had crocheted for me before I was born. I would make the three-hour trip half asleep, face stuck to the sweaty vinyl seat covers, but would swiftly awaken when Bess proclaimed, "We're crossin' the bridge!" She meant the small but magical bridge that took us into Ocean City, my childhood Bora Bora. There's nothing that can compare to sleeping in the back of your parents' car without a worry in the world, secure in the knowledge that you will wake to the smell of ocean breeze. I think that is what makes my mother cry every Christmas Eve when she hears "Silent Night." She misses that feeling of safety her parents gave her.

The summer I was nine, we all went to Ocean City (where else?) with five families we knew from the neighborhood community pool. Days were spent jumping waves and nights were spent walking the boardwalk, where we were treated to the smell of the famous Thrasher's French Fries, deep-fried in peanut oil, and Fisher's caramel corn, a buttery, blissful aroma that permeated the humid nighttime air and could be inhaled from a block away.

One night, all 25 of us hooked up at a pizza joint where they served birch beer and pitchers of real beer for the adults. Two hours in, someone put a quarter in the jukebox to play that season's hit, Jim Croce's "Bad, Bad Leroy Brown."

That did it. Our entire group of adults and children jumped up on top of the tables, Bess having initiated the rumpus with her verbal cajoling and spirited hand tugging, and we danced up there until the song was over. It was a great memory and is an even better philosophy. As Bess says, "I only danced on tables about a half dozen times. Everyone should do it! It's fun."

Annual Ocean City, MD family vacations

Annual Ocean City, MD family vacations

The dancing on the tables in Ocean City, MD crowd circa 1974

On the Craziest Place She Ever Danced

"This place called the Alcazar in downtown Baltimore. You would walk on the floor and dance with anyone you'd see. They had jitterbug music, and they would grab you and spin you around. But Christ, they didn't know when to quit. I'd yell, 'Stop! I'm gettin' sick!' Some guys thought they could dance, but all they could really do was spin you around."

On Dancing Shoes

"I wore five-inch heels, and so did my friend, but then she'd bring her driving shoes—her loafers. We'd laugh at those damn brown loafers from the time we got in the car. She said they made her drive better."

On Her Beverage of Choice

"No soda. We drank liquor—VO and 7 Up. It was $1.50 to get in, and the drinks were a dollar a piece. No martinis, none of that fancy stuff. The fanciest drink we had back then was a whisky sour. Nowadays at bars, they throw three liquors in one drink. That's not necessary."

On the Guy Who Spiked Her Drink One Night
"I should have knocked him against the wall. I was sick the entire day after."

On 52 Weeks of Dancing
"We went every Saturday night of the year! And sometimes, we would even do Friday night dances."

On What Made a Good Dance
"The fella you were with."

On Dancing at 88
"I can't walk, let alone dance on barstools anymore."

On Dancing and Not Driving
"My best friend, Shirley, and I were about 17, and we went dancing at this place called the Blue Mirror on Charles Street in Baltimore. We were dressed to the nines. This was a swanky place where guys went for pickups, but I wasn't at the age to drink. We met these two guys and went to this bar in the country so we could get served. We went to the ladies' room and when we came out, the guys were gone. We got dumped. We had no idea how we were going to get home, so Shirley and I went outside and she stuck her thumb out to hitchhike and a big, loud Greyhound bus stopped for us. The driver was the nicest man. When the bus pulled down my street, it lit up half the neighborhood. My mom was at the top of the steps in her

nightgown. She yelled, 'Where have you been?' and I told her I'd been out dancing. My mom said, 'You went dancing on a Greyhound bus?' She woke up my dad and said, 'Harry, there she is. Look at her. That hussy came home on a Greyhound bus after she went out.'"

Chapter 7
Lesson Seven
Death Has Its Light Moments

The days of my father's wake and funeral were a blur, except for "The Hair Affair," as we call it.

The first night of the viewing, Bud, Mom and I went into the parlor area of the funeral home to pay our private respects a few minutes ahead of the open visitation. We were all a bit freaked out as we approached Dad's coffin. It's really weird to see someone you've known your whole life dead. Then, you touch them. I couldn't understand why his hands were so cold, given the fact that it was 95 degrees outside. I was 30 years old at the time. *Other people's parents die*, I thought, *not my parents*. The whole situation felt surreal. Suddenly, Bess loudly chirped, "That doesn't look like him! His hair looks terrible. Bonnie, give me a comb."

She started running her fingers through his hair. *Holy sh*t, has she lost her mind?* I thought. Like a little kid taking orders from her first-grade teacher, I fumbled Mom's pocketbook open to look for something to comb his hair with. I found one of those timeless five-inch black plastic combs, and although I was filled with the intense fear that someone was going to see this crazy woman going to town on a corpse's hair or that Dad would miraculously sit up and tell her to back off, I gave it to her. I watched mutely as she aggressively pawed at his head. Then I looked at Bud, and he looked back at me, and we both burst out laughing. "Jesus Christ, Mom, would you leave the poor man alone?" I finally said.

"Wouldya let him have a little peace? People are going to think you're crazy," my brother added.

"Well, I don't care," barked Bess. "It doesn't look like him in there."

On Hair and Death
"I saw on TV there was this dead person they dug up after a bunch of years, and he had no clothes, but his hair had grown. I bet your father's hair is still growing. His hair is probably all over his face by now."

On Visiting the Cemetery
"I went to visit your dad, and I fell on top of the grave. Christ, I swear he was trying to pull me in."

On Being Cremated
"I don't know if I want to be cremated because your father may not recognize me."

On Organ Donation
"I'm afraid to sign up for that because, Christ, knowing my luck, I'd come back without an eye."

On Sudden Death

"I'm going to take that [allergy] pill, and so if I die tonight, just shove me wherever you want to."

On Dying While I'm Away

"Go away and have a great time. Enjoy yourself and don't worry about me. If I die, I'll tell them to put me on ice until you get back."

On Dying and Dishes

"I'm tired tonight. I didn't unload the dishwasher and left a few dishes in the sink. If I die, please unload the dishwasher, and don't leave the dishes in the sink."

On Obituaries and Cancelling *The Baltimore Sun* after a 60-Year Subscription

"I don't need it anymore. Everyone I know is dead."

On Dreaming about Our 88-Year-Old Neighbor Who Just Died

"I had a dream about John. He was standing in my living room, and I said to him, 'You're dead.' He said, 'I am?' Then I said, 'You better go home and tell your wife.'"

On Going to Ocean City as an Octogenarian

"I didn't see anyone I knew at Ocean City. Christ, that's because they're all dead."

On Unflattering Nail Polish

"Look at this nail polish on me. It looks like a dead person's nails. Just get Millie to do my hair, and I can die now because I'm ready to be laid out." Millie is the hairdresser who washes, dries, teases and loads Bess's hair with hairspray every Thursday. "Tell your dad to move over," she continued, "because I'm comin' in!"

On Death during a Pandemic

"Did you know people who die are being buried in whatever clothes they died in? Christ, I better go put on some high heels."

Chapter 8
Lesson Eight
Love Is for the Birds (and the Cats, Dogs and Whales)

Everyone says loving others begins with loving yourself, but Bess believes it starts with kittens and babies—gotta love 'em both. Because of Bess's love for cats, when I was a kid, I often searched for any cat I could find on the streets. They made me happy, and I wanted to bring them all home because I knew my mom and I shared the same love for animals.

I once found a full-grown cat a mile and a half away from my house. I scooped it up and lugged its squirmy little body all the way home. It was clearly someone else's cat, and my mom made me take it back, but it was worth a try. Mostly, she waved in anything I could find, except rats, mice, snakes and squirrels.

But soon, I had my own cat. I found him in my Christmas stocking in 1973, a six-week-old, gray-and-white striped kitten my parents bought for $15 at the local pet store. I named him Jason Kris Kringle Lorber. He was my buddy, but when we moved three years later, he didn't come home one night. I cried for days.

Three months later, we got a call from our old neighbor that Jason was hanging out under our backyard steps back in Baltimore. He had gotten lost at our new house and walked 24 miles, all the way back to our old house, looking for us. He was scrawny and sick, but we got Jason back to himself in no time with a little love from Mom and me. Bess always reiterates that she liked Jason because he was a clean cat. Come to think of it, as my girlfriend pointed out, what other kind of cat would survive in Bess's house?

The family pet, Jason, who trekked 24 miles to find our old home

Another time, my mom and I found a tiny baby bird in our driveway that must have fallen out of a tree. It looked like a mini version of E.T. and was minutes from sure death. We used an eyedropper to feed the puny little thing dry cat food moistened with water, and before we knew it, that bird grew feathers and filled out into a beautiful robin. After that, the bird would sit in the palm of my hand and let me snuggle it.

One day while I was doing just that, it flew away on its own like a child leaving for college. As I was expressing my heartbreak at the little creature's abrupt departure, Bess reminded me that the bird leaving was parallel to the relationship between a mother and child. "God only lends us our children; they're not ours to keep," she said. It was the first time I truly felt a twinge of what motherhood might feel like. That little bird was my first real experience of having a life depend on me for survival.

Over the years, Bess would often share her perspective on two major milestones of motherhood: first, the realization that you are forever a mom, and second, the indescribable void you feel once your children move out and leave the nest. Although she loves babies more than she loves kittens, her advice on preparing for a child went like this: "Make sure you're ready, 'cuz once they're here, you can't shove 'em back." I still share that facetious advice with everyone considering having a child because it's both funny and, well, true.

To this day, Mom frequently shares the pain and loneliness she experienced when I went away to college, describing her house as a tomb. She recalls the dark, wintry Friday nights when my dad would be out shooting darts with his league at the American Legion Hall while she sat at home in the living room rocking chair reading *The Baltimore Sun*. That was when our scraggly old, half-eared-from-a-catfight Jason seemed to intuitively recognize her sadness and would hop on her lap to comfort her. She still regularly talks about our kitty lovingly and affectionately, reflecting bluntly on his untimely death when some wild animal "bit off his balls" one night.

Although Jason was our last family pet, Bess remained fond of animals as years passed. After Jason's demise, she just didn't want to deal with the mess or be tied down, she explained—she had too many parties and dances to go to. But that love and sense of connection Bess holds for kitties and critters was reaffirmed recently.

A few years ago, my family and I rescued the best cat we ever had. Her name was Winnie, and unbeknownst to us, she was dying with a rare disease called Feline Infectious Peritonitis. We only had her for nine weeks when I had to put her to sleep, and I'd just walked into the house from saying goodbye when my phone rang. Through tears, I looked down at the caller ID. It said "Mom." Bess hadn't called me on the phone for at least 15 years. She had told me she stopped calling because she knew I was busy, and so now she waited for everyone to call her. To this day, she only calls for emergencies, and that's if she remembers.

I froze in fear for a second. Was something wrong? But when I said hello, what I heard was, "How's the cat?" After 15 years of birthdays, illnesses, deaths of humans and three presidential elections, her call to me was prompted by a dead cat.

On Birds, Bees and Brothels

For the 40 years since my family moved from the city, Bess has lived on a wooded lot. When I wasn't bringing them in myself, unwanted visitors like squirrels and mice often made their way into the house to be greeted by screams and swipes from the broom. One time, a squirrel got in and tore the house apart, gnawing at the wood trim, tearing up the curtains and turning on the stereo before dropping dead in Bess's favorite Ocean City beach bag. That stunk, literally and figuratively.

Another night, a window was left open, and a bird flew in the house. Bess managed to get it into the back room and opened the window there, but it wouldn't leave. Mom waited and waited and finally said to her new feathered friend, "I'm done waiting for you. I'm tired. I'm going to bed. You're on your own." The next day, it was gone.

Bess likes a nice backyard with lots of flowers, especially petunias, but as old age took away her green thumb, she switched to cascading plastic petunias in hanging pots. Even so, eating oatmeal and watching the wildlife in the morning is still her thing. She often tells me about the big, fat bird she sees every day and the chubby squirrel that can somehow jump six feet from tree to tree. In the spring and summer, my mom gives me daily updates on the mama birds who make nests in her flower baskets; the one that nests in the wreath on her front door even dives at her head.

One summer, there was a flurry of bird activity in the artificial flower basket that hangs from her deck. Babies were born in that basket, and weeks went by with birds flying in and out, in and out, like there was something really good in there.

"Bon," Bess told me one day, "You can't believe the amount of birds flying in and out of my bird basket every day. I don't know what's going on in there, but I really think it's a whorehouse for birds."

On Critters in Someone Else's Attic
"Did you hear about Miss Joan's house?" Bess asked me.

"No, what happened?"

"She's having a terrible time," Bess explained. "She has Cancuns living in her attic."

"She has what living there?"

"Cancuns, and they've made a mess! Those Cancuns can do a lot of damage, and they're mean. Ooh, I get chills just thinkin' about it."

"I think you mean raccoons," I replied.

"Yes, that is what I said," she answers. "Cancuns."

On Bouffants and Birds
"Christ, I went out to sit in the chair in the driveway because it was a beautiful day, and the next thing I know, a bird came down and sat on my head. He started trying to make a nest in my hair."

On Considering Feeding the Birds on the Deck
"I'd love to but forget that. They'll sh*t all over my house."

On Sharing a Coffin with the Dogs
"If [your Chihuahua] Max, [your brother's Maltese] Taffy and I die at the same time, you can bury them with me!"

On Ants, Critters She Hates
"I hope no one hears me, but when I see them in the kitchen, I call them little bastards."

On a Whale Breaching Offshore in Ocean City during the Pandemic
"I think with this damn quarantine, it sees there aren't people on the beach, and it's upset."

On My Howling Cat and My Daughter Who Was Missing Her Boyfriend during a Pandemic

"Boy, you got two of 'em in heat. That's no good."

On My 18-Year-Old Cat Rosie

"How is Susie?" Bess asked.

"I don't know how Susie is, but Rosie is fine," I replied.

On My Sick, 18-Year-Old Cat Who Survived Our Chihuahua

"How's the dog?" Bess asked.

"The dog has been dead for about a year, and the cat is next," I told her.

Chapter 9
Lesson Nine
Dress Your Bess-t and Rock the High Heels!

irst impressions are everything, according to Bess. It doesn't matter what words come out of your mouth; your fashion statement is more important. Appearance exemplifies your Bess-t self. If you were a fashion maven, you could be a screaming idiot and still be golden in Bess's eyes. From the earliest I can remember, Bess would critique people's hair, makeup and wardrobe with the intensity of a teenage girl stalking her ex-boyfriend on Instagram. There were no excuses for a slovenly appearance. You could be dying inside or already be dead and laid out, and it didn't matter. You always had to be rocking it on the outside.

Good hair was just as vital as fashion and shoes. For decades, Bess has had a standing Thursday appointment at 3:30 pm with Millie at Brenda's Beauty Boutique to get her hair washed, set, teased and sprayed. All in, it's about a 25-minute process from start to finish. It didn't matter if she'd had a stroke, recent stitches or a mental breakdown—if it was six degrees below zero or in the midst of a threatening apocalypse. To this day, that appointment ranks above any other in Bess's world, so it's no surprise that she's already made arrangements for a funeral hair appointment with Millie when the time comes.

Now, about those all-important shoes. When Bess was 87, I helped her clean out and condense all of her closets. As we went through her collection, she revealed that each set of heels— black, white or silver, three or five inches in height—had a different story associated with it. As she pulled out each pair, she'd share its story and the outfit she wore with them. Some had multiple stories, and all were keenly associated with good or bad parties or dances.

She routinely wore a four-inch, black patent leather pair to dances at the American Legion Hall, a venue she frequented with my dad every Friday night, and danced until "God Bless America" came on. This was the signature party-is-over song that ended with the house lights coming up to indicate it was time to go home. Sometimes, the ride home required an occasional nap on the side of the road. Bess showed me another pair of black faux leather pumps; these she wore to one of my dad's Christmas work dances because they perfectly completed her velvet holiday ensemble. They weren't only footwear; they were good friends.

On Heels

"I love high heels. They make your legs look good. I have short, stubby legs, so I need them. I have a friend who is 93 who still wears them. She looks like she's gonna fall and wobbles every step she takes, but they still look good on her."

A few weeks later, she told me this same friend fell and broke her ankle. About a month after that, she told me the same story again about her 93-year-old friend's high heels. I said with a little frustration, "Ma, you told me that story last month, and you told me she broke her ankle."

"I know I told you that," she snarked, "but she got her cast off, and she's wearing them again."

On Physical Therapy and Heels

"My lady who does therapy told me today my shoes aren't appropriate. Christ, they were only my little black sandals with two-inch heels."

On Her New Shoes

"Look at my shoes! I bought two pairs."

"I know, I bought them for you at Kohls," I reminded her.

"You have a cold?" she replied. "Drink some orange juice."

On the Dangling Pinky

When Bess wears open-toed shoes, an interesting phenomenon always occurs on both feet: her smallest toe sticks out. My brother and I call it the pinky toe scenario. That toe is always painted, but it is also always dangling. One day, I asked, "Hey Mom, why does that toe stick out?"

"Because it's too short for my shoes," She said matter-of-factly.

"They've stuck out all my life."

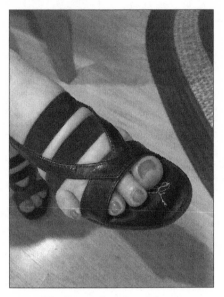

The famous, hanging pinky toe

On Getting Your Nails Done

"I think all women should get their nails done. I will do without food before I let my hair and nails go. This week I have orange nail polish on, and I got a lot of compliments on it."

Bess's favorite nail salon is owned by an Asian man, and all the nail technicians are also Asian, many from China. Whenever I come visit for a few days, we get our nails done and then grab a bite to eat. One day, in the middle of our pedicures and callous removals, she asked me three times if I was in the mood for Chinese food. "I could eat some Chanese, how about you?" she said in her strong Baltimore accent that often substitutes *ah* for *i*.

"Yes, Mom, that sounds good," I told her.

"I'm in the mood for Chanese, aren't you?" she repeated a little later.

"Okay, Mom, that sounds good," I replied again, hoping she'd switch subjects.

"I can't remember the last time I had Chanese," she said before beginning to bumptiously quiz the nail technician working on her feet. "How do you say your name? How come you didn't take one of those American names like all the others do? Do you like American food? Why doesn't the owner smile?"

On Judge Judy's New Hairdo
"She looks terrible. She looks a hundred years old."

On My Nephew's Haircut
"I don't like it. He looks like Kim Jong-un."

On My Daughter Doing Her Makeup for Her over Thanksgiving
"I guess I look okay. Actually, I look like a hooker."

On Not Being Dressed When the Physical Therapist Came
"I looked like a scum bum." I did not know what that meant, so I looked it up, and it's defined as what someone looks like after an epic night of drinking.

On Not Being Dressed When the Occupational Therapist Was Coming

"I look a mess, but it's not like I have a date with John Wayne. Is he dead yet?"

On Baseball Players' Looks on the Field These Days

"They dress terribly now with their long hair. I think they should have theirs cut. With those damn pigtails hanging down, you can't see their faces. They come on the field with all that jewelry and odd socks. In our day, you were a cupcake if you wore jewelry."

On Wearing Your Sunday Best

"We used to wear gloves and hats to church to show respect. Today, they dress terrible. The girls have their dresses up to their ass with a hundred holes in their dungarees, and they pay big money for that."

On My Daughter's Distressed Jeans

"Where did you get those jeans? Christ, they must have cost you $60. I would have cut holes in them for you for free."

On Cosmetic Surgery

"Christ, people get facelifts today like they're buyin' a new hat."

On Purple Hair

"It looks terrible. I think they should keep the hair they have."

Chapter 10
Lesson Ten
Life Is One Big Connection

One thing I learned from Bess is that memories are very powerful, and people and places make those memories. Despite her fading recollection, there are vivid, simple moments that have defined her happiness. Nowadays, I listen for hours to her reminiscing. It's as if she would do anything to relive those events for one more day, even her mother's Sunday family dinners that she and all her siblings were required to attend with their spouses. Bess believes today's generations do not invest the time to make connections, and to her, that is sad for the world.

"I think they are missing a lot," she says. "I don't think they appreciate family time as much. They don't have big turkey dinners. My mother had everything—stuffed chicken, roast beef, a freshly baked pound cake. When your dad and I were dating and had an argument, I would tell him, 'Don't come to my house on Sunday,' and he would get so mad. He didn't want to miss out on the dinner, but screw him. It was his own damn fault."

Perhaps she has a point. Today, those Sunday family dinners have been replaced with things like all day out-of-state soccer tournaments with a pit stop between games at Chick-fil-A or Panera Bread, or an all-day Netflix binge. Quite frankly, I can't imagine spending every weekend at my parents. I would have been divorced a long time ago if that had been a weekly requirement. But I do get the importance of family time. My daughter often professes that our family is an independent family. To clarify, she means we go off in our own directions a lot, and that is a good thing (I think). We have our own goals, thoughts and hobbies, but we also know how to blow out a Christmas Eve party together and that we are threaded like an oven mitt for eternity. We just choose our meeting spots instead of making it a standing calendar event.

But for Bess, those regular rituals like weekly family dinners, dances or visits to the shore gave those memories time to sink in deeper than the butter in one of her mom's scratch cakes. Everyone she talks about is connected to a sparkling detail, a glistening moment, favorite occasion or funny story. They are the shiny gems of her life. I think what she means to convey about these special moments is: *Savor them. Embrace them and remember them always, because at some point, there will be few new memories to make.*

On Ocean City, Her Connected Place

Hands down, my mother's favorite vacation spot will always be Ocean City, Maryland. All of her best memories seem to have happened there, including meeting my dad, bringing us kids there as babies, visiting with crazy friends after becoming empty nesters, hosting Christmas in July parties on the balcony of their condo and giving her grandchildren a chance to create their own memories of the shore. In my mother's eyes, there's no beach resort that can compare to Ocean City.

"You can take all those Caribbean islands and fancy places; just give me Ocean City," she says. "Best beaches and place in the world as far as I am concerned. It is a vacation spot for families, and they don't make 'em like that anymore." In my experience, it's also a place to feel safe and part of a community, a place where you can bump into friends from home, a place where memories are made and relived.

On NYC Being Almost as Good as Ocean City

To Bess, her trips to New York City are the runner-up to her memories from Ocean City—especially her honeymoon. There is a true twinkle in her eye as she speaks of that magical time. Buck was a big game show watcher, so my parents went to see a live game show as part of their stay in the Big Apple.

To add to the excitement, my father was chosen from the audience to participate in the show. If he answered the questions right, he'd go home with $500. Dad did well on the first few questions, but when the final one came, he wasn't able to answer it. Bess still remembers what it was. She may not remember the name of the game show or what she did yesterday, but she can tell you what she wore, hat, gloves and all, and that he missed the final question about what the little black dots are called on common six-sided dice. (For the curious among you, they're called pips.)

Now, 65 years later, Bess's love of the city has infected our whole family. For a few winters, we'd all go there together to see a show and have a fun weekend. I lived in Long Island, New York, while my mom and brother still live in Bel Air, Maryland. Mom and Buddy's family would take the Megabus, a double-decker, express service that brought them right into Times Square. My two nephews and niece usually had their eyes closed for the trip, and most of the bus riders did as well, as the service took off from the Baltimore station at around 7 am.

Bess is loud, and she has always been this way. In high school, my friends called us "The Loud Family." I never realized how noisy we were until college, when I occasionally stayed at other people's homes and experienced the discrepancy in overall volume firsthand upon re-entering my house afterward. Bess is also chatty, and invariably, on that early bus to New York, she was chatting away while everyone else was snoozing.

"Bess, you're being too loud. Everyone can hear you," my nephew Justin once told her.

"Christ, this bus is no fun. You can't even talk on it," Bess told him.

Getting off the bus, my brother said to my mother, "Let me put on your coat."

"No," Bess responded, "I don't want a Coke."

The Cemetery Connections

There's a massive cemetery in Baltimore called Most Holy Redeemer that Mom asks us to take her to sometimes. She goes there to visit my dad's parents and to see her friend Fran (short for Francis), who she dated after Dad passed away. Fran was a bachelor his whole life, but he loved Bess and wanted to marry her. Bess never stopped loving my dad; she has always said she never wanted to get remarried because she was afraid she wouldn't be with my dad on the other side. I think that is sweet.

Fran died when he was 87, and Bess would visit Fran's tombstone in Most Holy Redeemer Cemetery when she could. Often, it was my brother who took her. Once in the cemetery, he watched her stop at each of the tombstones she passed, moving in close to read the names. Every few feet, she would stoop and squint at the name on the stone. "Ma, what are ya doin'?" Bud asked. "What are you lookin' for?"

"Oh, I'm looking at all the headstones because I want to see if I know any of 'em," She replied. "I think I dated some of these dead people."

Dinner and the Google Death Search

One summer night, I took Bess and her best friend Betty out to dinner for some "Chanese food." Talk about a challenge. Bess can't walk or hear and Betty can't see, but they are a riot when they get together. I call them "Double Trouble, Double Fun."

Here's the usual scenario with Bess when leaving the house: she's got her cane in one hand, five-pound purse on her forearm and a paper cup with iced tea in the other hand as she walks the eight steps down from the front door. It's a dicey maneuver, but it doesn't matter how many times we beg, plead, warn and even yell at her; that's the way she does it. As she says, "You gotta go somehow. Just give me the little black pill."

When we got to the restaurant, chatter turned into reminiscing, which turned to another classic topic: wondering about death. Bess mentioned a mutual friend, and Betty said, "I wonder if she is still alive."

After naming their sixth person, I said, "Give me their full names and the town they lived in." At that, I pulled out my phone and started fiercely researching their buddies. Weirdly, whenever I found one of their obituaries, it was like striking gold. It was a sick thing, but I was so happy to be able to tell them the status of each of their friends—even if, unfortunately, the status kept coming back the same: *I'm sorry, but he's dead; I am so sorry, but she died, too.*

For each person we'd discuss, they'd gasp and feel terrible and sad, and then that would spark the inquiry into the next one. It was like I was watching a death pool in real-time. More than once, Bess would say, "How did I miss that one? I read the obituaries every day."

As morbid as it was, I was still weirdly glad to be helpful.

Chapter 11
Lesson Eleven
Moms Show Love Differently

The main pillar of my mom's existence and self-esteem was and still is food. To Bess, food equals love.

"Are you hungry? Are you thirsty? Please, eat something!" she pesters relentlessly. One day, during one of our deep conversations about her life, she explained that she learned this from her parents. "They never said, 'I love you' to us. The fact that they had three meals a day and ample food in the home said it loud enough," she told me.

I think back to my childhood and realize that I also lived this truth. Between the ages of seven and nine, I went through a stage of waking up nearly every night at 3 am to ask my mother for a waffle with powdered sugar and a glass of milk. Bess gladly got up, pulled out the portable toaster, waited two minutes for the waffles to pop up, spread butter on them so that it melted just right with the powdered sugar and then brought it upstairs to my bed.

I also remember numerous times that Friday lunchtimes in

grade school felt the way Starbucks in the morning does to me now. It was a happy, warm comfort that was most welcome! Some days, Bess would bring me in a McDonald's hamburger and french fries while the other kids suffered with bologna on white bread or a PBJ. None of the other moms did this, and some moms serving lunch duty that day were rolling their eyes. For sure, the Golden Arches were the talk of many dinner tables those nights.

As Bess has gotten older, orange juice has become the nectar of her existence. My mother has become a tad hard of hearing, but still, whenever I visit Bess and wake in the middle of the night to go to the bathroom, she still hears the creak of the 45-year-old wooden planks, even though they're covered by worn-down carpet. "How about some orange juice?" she'll ask me. According to Bess, orange juice is a cure-all.

"Mom," I'll say, "it's 3 am."

"That doesn't matter. You might be hungry or thirsty."

Come to think of it, many of our arguments have been over food. "Have a pretzel. Want some cold pears? Have a little Ovaltine. Drink some Coke." She's constantly trying to force-feed me, and any out-of-the-house event includes the regular staples: a small, red Igloo cooler packed with Cokes on ice, 12-ounce Styrofoam cups and cheese or peanut butter crackers. All of which she's sure I will need.

The annual Thanksgiving meal growing up was particularly gluttonous. We would have no fewer than six vegetable sides for the ginormous turkey as well as pre-scooped ice cream, ready to go on plates stored in the freezer to be served with a selection of pies. Then, two hours after finishing dessert, the leftovers would come back out with shrimp salad and more side dishes.

"Mom, stop with the food!" I'd moan.

Her response: "People are hungry."

Bess would also always try to rationalize the inherent value of junk food.

"Have an Oreo!"

"No, Mom, that's not good," I'd tell her.

"Why? It won't hurt you." Then, "Have some cake."

"Mom, I'm watching my weight."

"Well, the cake has eggs in it, and they are good for you."

The other thing that is "good for you" is taking a bath; if all else fails, just hop in the tub! Don't feel good? Take a bath. Had a long day? Take a bath. Stub your toe? Take a bath. Your boyfriend cheats on you? Take a bath. It's raining? Take a bath. Are you happy? Take a bath. There's a thumb up your ass? Take a bath. And you know what? A few years ago, I redid my entire upstairs and made sure to have a nice soaking tub installed, because goddammit, she is right!

Bess insists that orange juice and a bath are two things that will always make you feel more energized. I remember we were on the phone one night, and I asked how her day was. Again, the conversation turned to orange juice.

"I made a mistake and put orange juice on my cereal today," Bess told me.

"Okay. What was that like?" I asked. "Did you put it down the disposal?"

"No," Bess replied. "That orange juice is expensive. And it is so good for you, so I ate it. It wasn't too bad. A lot of cereal has fruit in it anyhow. Raisin Bran just came out with banana in it."

On Health Care

"You have a cold? Drink some orange juice."

On Giving Her Granddaughter Ice Cream for Breakfast

"It's good for her. It has milk in it."

On Eating Chocolate Instead of Using the Heimlich

"They say if you're choking to eat chocolate," Bess claimed.

"I think you mean if you have a bad cough," I said.

"I think you're right."

On My Husband's Request to Pass the Bread to Make Toast

"It's so nice that you would like to make a toast before we eat. Sure, go ahead. Let's hear it."

On a Sophisticated Wine Selection for Thanksgiving

"Would you like me to pick you up some Boone's Farm?"

On Not Having Any Beer in the Fridge

"It's Thanksgiving, and I don't even have a beer to offer anyone," Bess announced.

"Ma," I said, "No one is stopping over, and we don't need any beer."

"Well, I don't know what happened to the beer I had in the refrigerator."

"We threw that beer out a few years ago."

"Why did you do that?" she asked accusingly.

"Because it was super old and smelled like skunk beer," I explained.

"That beer was fine."

"Ma, how old was that beer?"

"Oh, I don't know. I bought it before your dad died."

"Ma, Dad died in 1995. That is worse than skunk beer."

"No, it wasn't," Bess maintained. "Beer never goes bad."

To My Daughter's Italian Boyfriend during a Facetime Introduction

"Italian people are nice. Do you eat a lot of spaghetti?"

On How to Feel Better after I Fired Someone and Learned My Dog Was Dying

"Go home and drink a nice, big, cold glass of milk. Then take a bath."

On Asparagus

"Ma," Bud asked, "where do you want to go to dinner?"

"I could go for some asparagus," Bess decided.

"Okay. We can go to Outback."

Buddy pulled up to the restaurant and parked, went around to get her out of the car, took her by the hand and made sure she had her cat cane. Then, they embarked on the slow walk to the restaurant. Bess looked up at him and said, "I can't wait for that crab cake."

Bud stopped in his tracks, turned to her and said, "Mom, you told me you were in the mood for asparagus. They don't sell crab cakes here!"

"Oh, I did?" she replied. "What restaurant are we at?"

So crab cakes it was. They got her back into the car and journeyed on to Bess's preferred destination.

On My Strange, Healthy Diet
"Christ, the next time I see you, I won't be surprised if you start to grow rabbit fur."

Chapter 12
Lesson Twelve
Educate Yourself, So You Don't Have to Take Sh*t You Don't Want To

Never depend on a man. That was the philosophy Bess repeatedly tried to instill in me throughout my childhood. But I was pretty skeptical about how she was able to provide that wisdom. Ironically, she clearly depended on my dad, at least financially.

When I grew older, she went back to work part-time as a retail salesperson in various clothing stores, and I remember her sharing dozens of stories over the years about how some of the "young girls" she worked with were stuck in life, meaning they had no formal education, were in bad relationships and had to take "sh*t from their husbands." She would say to me at least three times a week, "Get your education, make your own money and don't take any sh*t from anyone." The truth was, even though Bess depended on my father financially, she would never take any sh*t. I think she was a bit ahead of her time in this area.

She pounded this into my head so much that when I had my

daughter, instead of singing her the real words from *Sleeping Beauty's* "Some Day My Prince Will Come," I created my own personalized version. Holly got strange looks from friends and other parents when she would sing it at the top of her lungs:

> *Someday my prince will come,*
> *Someday my prince will come,*
> *After I go to college and get a good job,*
> *I promise I won't marry a slob!*

I held off sharing the real lyrics as long as I could. I don't think Holly knew them until she was 16.

My mother's self-esteem rested solely on her ability to take care of her children and show love through food, whereas women in today's world have a variety of elements they can use to fill up their self-esteem bag. Though Bess raised me to think and live independently, I find that in many ways, her belief system was somewhat torn between generations.

I am a professional woman who works between 50 and 65 hours a week, but when I go to visit my mom, she often asks if I iron my husband's clothes and fix him breakfast in the morning. Of course, my husband will play into this and tells her, "Oh Mom, I barely get anything to eat, and I'm always fending for myself." She immediately empathizes with him.

Remember, this is the same mom who ironed and laid out my dad's clothes every night and woke early in the morning to make him breakfast. But instead of letting it bother me, I just think back to *I Love Lucy* reruns and how well they show the ways women of that decade were relegated to taking care of the husband and home, invariably failing any time they tried to step outside of that role. What the heck? My, how things have changed since then. I can only imagine what would happen if someone had told my daughter she had to attend a home economics class and hone her dusting skills as a requirement to graduate high school.

For the majority of my childhood, Bess was a homemaker who started to work part-time as a sales associate in a women's fashion store when I turned nine. She was there for me when I needed her to be: every birthday and school event or for anything else I could ever ask for. I didn't spend a night away from her until 12 or 13, when I started having sleepovers.

My mom existed in a time period in which her needs were always ranked last, yet she strongly supported my ability to attend college. In fact, after I graduated, I learned my parents took out a second mortgage on their house to send me. With every report card, she told me how wonderful my "good marks" were and would end her praise with, "You are smart. Get your education, and don't ever depend on a man for anything. You can tell him to go to hell because you will be able to make your own money. You don't need to take anyone's sh*t."

She always encouraged me to nurture my confidence and self-reliance. Even to this day, she says, "Good for you. You don't need anyone for money. You earn your own money."

More from Bess on Independence

During our drives to the grocery store or hairdresser, I like to ask Mom a question or two to get her thoughts on current events. One of those conversations occurred after she took out a mailbox and nearly totaled her car, and then a few days later, she cut her hand and had to get six stitches. As we talked, I was trying to get her mind off of the sh*tty week and so threw out the most controversial topic I could think of to get her insight and to leverage a bit of her wisdom.

"Hey Bess, what are your thoughts on the Me Too movement?" I asked.

"I've had a very busy week and haven't had time to read the paper about that story," she replied.

Ahhhh. This is about as far away from a one-day story that you can get, Bess.

On Workplace Culture
"Does your boss kiss you on the cheek when he sees you? Mine used to all the time."

On Sexual Harassment in the Workplace
"Guys used to pinch our butts or snap our bra straps. There was nothing wrong with that."

On Midday Happy Hours
"Everyone had a fifth of whiskey stashed in their cabinets."

On Addressing Women Professionally
"They used to say, 'Hey sweetheart, how are you today, hon?'"

On Mixers
"Our boss would yell at us if we bought too many ginger ales

from the soda machine because other employees would know we were making drinks."

On Work Drinking
"We really only did this on Fridays when our boss would share his VO."

On the Horse Races
"My boss would sneak out every Friday afternoon after he gave us some VO."

On Ergonomic Chairs
"What are they?"

On What Not to Do with Your Lunch
"Ooh, I'll never forget," Bess said, immediately starting to laugh.

"One day, when I was working at ARMCO, the big boss downstairs was having a meeting in a conference room. In the middle of a serious talk, he saw noodles sliding down the windah. He got mad and called my boss and asked who threw the noodle soup out the windah. Christ, it was me. My boss came into our office and said, 'Who had chicken noodle soup for lunch today?' I said, 'Uh, that was me.' He snapped, 'Well, next time you throw it out the windah, make sure you throw it farther away from the building.' Christ, my work friends and I laughed for weeks about that one."

On the Office Slut
"This one girl, I think, screwed everyone in the office. She was foolin' around with one of the bosses who had big feet and all of these holes in his socks. To this day, I don't know what she saw in him."

On the Manager Who Supplied the Alcohol
"He was a great boss. He was the best I ever had."

On Sexual Harassment
"When my girlfriends and I would walk to the café at work, we had to pass the guys at the steel mill. I was always afraid I would get a piece of steel caught in my high heels. They would yell and whistle at us, 'Hey, you got great legs,' whistle, whistle. There was nothing wrong with that."

On Her Postpartum Depression with Her First Child
"I was taking care of my father, had just lost my mother, gave up my job and was stuck home all day with a baby. I thought I was losing my mind. I went to the doctor, and he told me I had combat fatigue and gave me a Valium."

On the Work Infirmary
"Christ, if we were tired or hungover, we would go down and take a nap. My boss didn't care."

On Equal Pay
"Men always got paid more than women. They did the same job."

Chapter 13
Lesson Thirteen
Hitch Your Wagon to a True Partner, Not Half an Ass

"Years ago, my friend used to say, 'Why buy the cow when you can get the milk for free?'" Bess says. When I was a teenager, she used that expression herself all the time with me. I have no idea if she was a virgin when she got married, and like all kids, I really don't want to know. But considering how many times she made this point, it sounds like there was no free-flowing milk before she got her ring.

"I don't think you should jump right into bed with a guy," she tells me. "These girls today have no sense. They need to respect themselves to get the respect back and get a gentleman."

On Relationships Today
"They do it all backwards. They're supposed to get married and have children. Now they screw before they kiss, and they have children who are old enough to be in the wedding by the time they eventually do get married."

On College

"It should be lights out at 11 pm, and girls should live in one dorm and the boys in the other. Parties are okay, but you don't need all of this all-night sex."

On Her Hoochie-Mama Aunts

"My two aunts really gave it away. The one never even wore underpants."

On Being More Like They Are in the Hallmark Movies: No Milk for Free

"I like that there is no sex in those movies but get tired of having to watch them for two hours just to see them finally kiss. Kiss her already! And all the guys wear toupees. None of their hair is real. They all look the same with that hairline. Can't you tell?"

On One of Her Dates When She Was 19

"He was so cute. His hair was all slicked back, he was dressed nice and he had a good job and a nice car. On the second date, he told me we were going somewhere real nice. Christ, it was a wrestling match. Here I was all dressed up, and I had to sit there for three hours watching these people roll around. After that, I said to myself, Christ, I'm not going out with him anymore."

On Hallmark's Christmas in July Marathon

"Christ, I'm going to be tired of Christmas by the time it gets here."

On the Royal Wedding of Harry and Meghan

"I'm not waking up at no six o'clock in the morning to watch that. Besides, Christ, they've been screwing for a year already."

On the Neighborhood Brawl with the Woman Who Gave Up Free Milk

"Rumor is our old neighbor and the girlfriend he was living with got in a fight, and he threw her out on the front porch without her teeth and wouldn't give them back. She called the cops. I wouldn't put up with that sh*t."

On the Royals Naming Their Baby Archie

"I used to date an Archie. He was the nicest guy. I would visit him at the bar he worked at, and he would give me free pretzels. I liked him a lot until I found out he had a wife and two kids."

On Men Today

"I think men are terrible today. They are overly sexed and out looking for free sex wherever they can get it."

On Women Today

"They are just as bad as the men."

On Men and Their Asses

If men aren't up to par as partners, they should be shipped out, according to Bess. "Some guys paint a room half-assed. Some don't pick up anything or help their wives. Some go out to bars when they want to. They get married and think they don't have to do things anymore, and they become half-assed. Their actual ass is there, but they are half-assed in their head and how they do things."

On Uncle Phil
"I'm getting disgusted with Uncle Phil," Bess said.

"Who is Uncle Phil?" I asked her, confused.

"You know, the guy on TV."

"You mean Dr. Phil?"

"Yes," she informed me. "All those women go on his show with their half-assed husbands telling their stories about how they do this and that to them. They should throw their asses out."

"I am going to post that one on Facebook," I told her, laughing.

"Don't do that, or Uncle Phil might call my house!"

On the Baltimore Criminal Who Was Convicted of Assaulting a Young Girl
"Someone should cut off his balls. Give me the knife. I'll do it and shove them in his mouth."

On Remembering Something My Husband Said That Was Not Half-Assed
As Holly grew up and became an adult, she used to love to talk to my mom on the phone. She always knew she had to allow for at least an hour, but it was worth it for the funny things Bess

would say to her. The conversations always ended on my daughter's love life. My mother loves romance, as her addiction to the Hallmark Channel reveals, and her advice always ends with her "don't depend on a man" mantra. One night, she shared a good memory of a man who was, thank goodness, anything but half-assed.

"Holly, I remember your dad gave a speech when he won that baseball award, and it was the nicest thing," Bess told her. "He went on to say that of all the pitches he made, the best one he ever made was marrying your mother." And then she paused and said, "Hmmmm."

"What's wrong, Bess?" my daughter asked.

"What's her name again?"

A few months later, we were chatting about anniversaries as she and my dad would've been celebrating their 68th if he had still been alive.

"How long have you and John been married now?" Bess asked.

"We will be married 30 years in October," I said.

"Gosh, really?" she replied. "Do you still like him?"

Chapter 14
Lesson Fourteen
All This Modern Technology
F*cks Things Up

B ess doesn't get technology. She still looks for the Yellow Pages if she needs to find a phone number. It doesn't matter that its thousands and thousands of pages have gradually whittled down to nearly nothing over the years. To her, it's still 1970, and if she needs to find a number, she's pulling out that book. Still, she has a love-hate relationship with her family's cell phones.

"That little machine you have is wonderful," she told me one day. "It helps you a lot. What does one of those little things cost?" But just a little while later, while waiting for dinner to be served at our favorite cozy restaurant, she flip-flopped. "I hate those doodads you all use," she criticized. She hates them because they are a distraction, and she believes they make people rude. "You can never have or finish a conversation with anyone anymore because of those damn cell phones."

Other concepts that come with technology are a stretch for

Bess, too, like ordering clothes and groceries online. But if you think about it, Amazon and Peapod are really electronic catalogs. Back in the '50s, everyone had an account at the local grocery store that would allow you to order groceries and have a delivery boy bring them to your home. When I try to explain to her how you can do this via computer, she simply says, "I don't have the equipment to do that."

Now, when I find she needs something she doesn't have, I whip out the "doodad" and order from Amazon while she tells me what she needs. Mesmerized by the ordering process, she'll inevitably ask, "What's this Amazon all about?" It has dawned on me that though it may seem that time and technology have outpaced her, the reality is that familiar processes have merely been revolutionized through technology.

The same goes for the concept of Google and online search. It's apparent that she has heard all the terminology, but she clearly can't make the connection between the words and their functionality. Although technology and all its ambiguous charms are beyond her grasp, Bess has still included it in her world—in her own way.

On the Weathergirl with the Long Arms

"Bon, I want to watch the weather. Let's see if the girl with the long arms is on. You have to see her. They are so long. Someone needs to tell her not to wear short sleeves. When she points at the weather map, it looks like she has an extension on her arm. Have you ever seen anyone with arms that long? And what is with that hair? She looks terrible. And her clothes. Maybe she bought them from that Amazon place."

On Her Friend's Computer That Had a Virus

"No wonder his computer got sick. You should see the dust in his apartment."

On My Tenacious Banging on My Computer Keyboard for Work

"Bonnie is on that thing doing her homework all day long and there are cords all over the place. I don't care what she does so long as long as she doesn't try to shove one of them in me."

On What You Get When You Cross Uber with Google

It was time. Bess's driving skills were starting to make us all nervous, and she really needed to stop driving for good.

"Ma," I said, "we can get you a service or a person who can come and take you wherever you want. Nails, hair, the dollar store, you name it."

"I don't want any damn service," she snapped. "That last girl you brought in here was a hillbilly. I don't want anyone in my house. I can take care of myself. I will figure it all out." And then she blurted out with gusto, "I know what I'll do! I'll Goober it."

Uber + Google = *Goober!*

On Top-Rated Drivers

On Thanksgiving 2018, we treated Bess to her first Uber ride. Her days of putting together a Thanksgiving feast for 20 people had been replaced by a family gathering at a restaurant. As we had a bit of a group with us, we ordered an UberXL, which sat up to six people. Lucky for us, we got a hip and friendly, award-winning driver who took his job very seriously.

He was proud to tell us he was the number-one-rated driver in the country or state; I can't recall which award he had won, but it was quickly clear why he'd won it. This driver opened the doors as we hopped in the car, put mints in the door handle pockets and offered us a phone charger with six different cords. He was cheerful even though he was working the holiday, and right away, my mother was hitting it off with her new friend, her first Uber driver.

Throughout the 20-minute ride, Mom kept bringing up Tyrell, my 27-year-old nephew Brandon's best friend, who is a police officer. Tyrell and Brandon have been friends since they could talk. Over the years, he has become like family to us. But over the course of the ride, it became clear as she talked to our driver that Tyrell was also my mom's sole point of reference for young men of color.

Halfway through the trip, Bess turned to us and said, "He looks just like Tyrell. In fact, he could be Tyrell's brother."

The driver chuckled and said, "Ma'am, I am not Tyrell's brother, but I am *a* brother."

Advice for Her Grandson

"Those phones aren't good. Do you read the *Reader's Digest*? You should."

On My iPhone's Dead Battery
"I have plenty of batteries at home. What size do you need? I think I even have a nine-volt."

Her Ultimate Doodad Advice
"Get rid of the phones, at least for a bit, and especially at the dinner table."

Despite her opinions on technology, I wish Bess had an iPhone to keep track of her contacts. I promised Bess I'd rewrite her black book of life connections, a five-by-eight-inch phone book that had all of her contacts for everything and anything Bess-related.

As I said it, it occurred to me how great having new technology was and how much time it saved. Believe it or not, it took me almost two days to get through the penned copy of my mom's black book, because my mom would read each of the names to me, and then we'd embark on a crazy debate about whether they were phonebook-worthy or not, my sort-of analogy to *Seinfeld*'s famous "sponge-worthy" episode.

"Okay, let's go," Bess started. "Hmm. Write down 'Alvin the painter.' Here's his number."

"Bess, who is Alvin?" I asked. "I've never heard you mention him."

"Oh, he's a painter that we used when we first moved up here."

"What, 42 years ago?"

"Yes, why?" she eyed me suspiciously.

"How old do you think he was back then?"

"Oh, I don't know, maybe in his 60's?"

"Ma, Alvin is not painting anymore," I told her. "In fact, I believe he isn't breathing anymore either."

"Hmmm. Okay. Let's go to the next one. BWI Airport."

"Bess, why in the world do you think you need the number of BWI Airport? When was the last time you called it?"

"When you were in college."

"I graduated in 1986," I reminded her.

"Bonnie, I may still need that number," Bess instructed me emphatically. "Okay, let's go to page four. Let me see here." Her finger swiftly moved from top to bottom, stopping at a line.

"Hmm—he's dead." A second later. "She's dead." Two seconds later. "*Dead, Dead, Dead.* This whole page is *Dead!*"

Moving on, Bess restarted, "Page five. Here is the tax guy at Harford County courthouse. I want to keep his number."

"Why? When was the last time you went to see him?" I wondered.

"Oh, I don't know, maybe 1980? Hmmm. Well, let me see. I guess you can get rid of that one."

Chapter 15
Lesson Fifteen
Stop This Politics Stuff and Be Nice

According to Bess, "There's a lot of sh*t going on in the world these days. Everything is quite political." My mom believes the world has gone a bit sideways and wishes for simpler times where people were kinder and more focused on the positive. "People have to get back to religion and caring for each other. Dreams of world peace?" Bess says. "Just make peace in your home. People are nuts. They don't know how to value things anymore, and it's a shame, because life is too short. They need to appreciate what they have. I know we did."

Bess has a lot to say on ways to minimize world chaos. Her philosophy? Eat and be merry. As she explains, "When I was young and married, we had a big dinner every Sunday. All of the grown kids would come to my mom and dad's house, and my mom would wake up at the crack of dawn to whip up homemade cakes. We would all crowd around a little table to eat. Good memories. Good peace."

But when asked her thoughts on our leadership, she heeds

her own recommendations and keeps things apolitical. Instead, Bess's priorities regarding political figures follow her philosophies expressed in Lesson Eight. Literally.

On President Trump
"I like when he gives the thumbs up."

On President Trump's Hair
"I think he could change the style, but he is covering up a bald spot."

On the Cutest President
"President Kennedy. His wit and personality were funny."

On the Best-Dressed First Lady
"Jackie Kennedy. She always wore suits, had good-looking clothes and an outfit for every sport, like jumping off horses."

On the Least Trustworthy President
"The guy with the nice hair whose wife dressed terrible. You know who I mean. The womanizer."

On What President She Could Have the Most Fun With
"Trump. I think I'd have fun with him."

On Who Was the Nicest President
"Truman. By the way, is he dead yet?"

On Trump's Presidency
"It's a shame he has gotten so fat."

On the Former First Lady

"That Elania [sic] looks like she hates the whole world. Trump holds her hand everywhere, but at home, he probably yells at her."

On Then-Presidential Candidate Biden

"He looks half dead."

On President Biden Falling Down the Steps When Attempting to Board Air Force One

"It reminded me of the time I fell on the ice in eighth grade in front of a full school bus of laughing preteens," I said to Bess.

"Oh, I know," she sympathized. "That was so terrible. Well, you know why he fell, don't you?"

"No, why?" I asked, puzzled.

"I think he had on new shoes because every time he tried to get up, he kept falling, and that's because they were slippery on the bottom. You know, shoes are like that when they are new," she explained, as if she had spoken with the President herself.

On Inviting President Biden to Her Tea Party with Her Friends

"Christ, Bonnie is inviting so many people tomorrow, she is probably inviting the President," Bess said.

"Do you want her to invite him?" Asked her aide, Leigh Ann.

"Christ, no!" said Bess. "I'd have to wake him up and get him dressed."

On Foreign Policy
"That Kim Jong-un, I don't trust him. He looks mean, and I hate his haircut."

More on Foreign Policy
"Why can't we eat Kit Kats anymore?" Bess asked me. "The President had a speech today about them. He said we have to ban Kit Kats from the country."

"Hmm," I responded, slightly confused. "You think maybe he said ban TikTok?"

"No, he said Kit Kats. But maybe you're right. I thought it was strange that Kit Kats were that important that they would be in a speech by the President and he would make a point to say we couldn't eat 'em anymore."

On Osama bin Laden
"Did you know he wore a cowboy hat?"

On Who Was the Smartest President
"None of them. They all play guessing games."

Chapter 16
Lesson Sixteen
Be Patient with the Quirky and Weird

I started taking notes on my mom's comments, colorful philosophies and witty wisdom when she turned 80. Through the years, the misinterpretations and misunderstandings resulting from Bess's softening hearing and recollection mixed with her sharpening resolve and straightforwardness have kept me, my brother and our families very entertained.

It dawned on me that someday, due to the accumulation and volume of saucy stuff she says or eventually, because of my own aging mind, I would forget. And she makes us laugh, so why not memorialize this world, according to Bess? It would be sort of like a live eulogy that went on for pages.

On Chicken Pot Pie with Cheese and Keys
I hated chicken pot pie as a kid but learned to like it as an adult. My mom used to make it from scratch, even the crust. For a few months, she had been talking about how she could go for some chicken pot pie, so I asked her for the recipe, made several for

her and froze them. In fact, I even ordered some jars of her favorite chowchow, a sort of sweet and spicy relish used in the South, to put on top of it. Of course, it was purchased from none other than Amazon.

During one of my visits, I asked, "How are those pot pies? Let's have one." I popped one in the oven and took out a jar of the relish.

"Oh my gosh!" Bess exclaimed. "Where'd ya find this chow-chow? I've looked all over for it."

"Well, Mom, I got it from Amazon!" I told her.

"That Amazon thing again. It's like the Sears catalog but bigger."

We started to eat. The pot pie was good, but something about its taste was off.

"I think I put in too many peas, Mom," I said. "I hope it's good."

"You said you put cheese in it?" Bess asked.

"No, Mom. I said I put in too many peas."

"You need my keys?" She started to reach for her purse.

"Oh, my God, Mom! I said I put in too many *peas. Peas!*"

A few weeks later, my brother texted me that she was eating

another one of the pot pies. I was so happy and texted him back that I would make her some more.

"She said it's good, but not as good as hers," he replied.

On My Daughter Having an Attitude on the Phone Once
"What's wrong with Holly, and why does she have an altitude?"

On My Postpartum Struggles after 42 Hours of Labor and a C-Section
"Why are you walking all hunched over like that? Stand up straight."

On the Show *Cops*
"I like the drunks without the teeth on that show. They're funny. I don't know how those cops catch them; they're all so fat."

On the 10 O'Clock News Anchor
"I think that lady went back to school for English class or somethin', as she couldn't say any words before, and she has gotten better. She is as cute as a button."

On the Charity Phone Solicitation She Received
"When I answered the phone, this stupid woman Amanda told me I was slower answering the phone than her husband was coming to dinner. Can you imagine? Those imbeciles."

On Her Aide's Current Shapeliness
"Did you used to be thin?"

On the Charity Mail Solicitations She Receives

"Christ, they put the same kid on that envelope every year. He's gotta be grown by now. They should either put a new photo on there or stop asking for money."

On the Retired Dentist Who Made Her False Teeth

"I loved my dentist. I want to write him a note, but I don't want his wife to think I'm trying to pick him up."

Mirror, Mirror on the Wall

"Hand me that brush and mirror," Bess asked me. She held the brush up to her face, thinking it was the mirror—the fancy kind with the handle like in the animated fairy tales. "This g*dd*mn thing doesn't even work."

On the Pandemic

"People are going around cleaning up every place after all this mess. Why the hell didn't they clean before we got this thing? I blame it all on dirt."

More on Dirt Causing the Pandemic

"People throw wrappers on the ground or put them in their pockets. That doesn't help."

On Getting a Vaccine for the Coronavirus

"I don't need any vaccine. I had a tetanus shot."

On Me Pulling Up Her Mask Every Time She Pulls It Down

"I don't understand why you keep putting that mask over my nose."

On Names

Over the last few years, family dinners with Mom have become
a challenge, especially when the group includes the millennial
generation's new girlfriends or boyfriends. Bess isn't good with
names, and the kids always warned their friends not to be
offended if she called them the wrong one.

For example, my niece has been dating her guy Cameron for
years, but to Bess, he is known as Camry, like the Toyota. And
when my daughter brought her boyfriend Jordan, who lived in
England, to Thanksgiving dinner, Bess introduced him to
everyone as George from Germany. When asked why she did
this, she laughed out loud and said, "Names are not my
strength."

On My Husband John and the Lunchmeat Man

"I've been meaning to tell you that there's this guy on TV that
looks like John," Bess informed me.

"Really?" I wondered to myself. "Hmm. A movie star, maybe?
Someone hot?"

"Yeah, he looks just like that guy on the lunchmeat commercial,"
she added.

"Mom, what commercial? What lunchmeat? Boar's Head?"

"No."

"Dietz & Watson?"

"No."

"Butterball?"

"No."

"Esskay?"

"No."

"Hormel?"

"No, the other one."

"Okay," I thought. Then I asked her, "What other lunchmeats are there?"

On My Brother's Benign Brain Tumor
"No wonder why you've acted crazy all these years. It's because you have that lump in your head!"

On Her Hearing
My ringtone is the strum, which is common on the iPhone. It is what it sounds like, a few chords of guitar strumming, but for Bess, it is also something else.

One day, I was helping her clean up in the kitchen, and my cell phone rang. She started to sing, "You put your right foot in, you put your right foot out, you put your right foot in, and you say get all about."

She saw me looking at her incredulously. "Don't you hear that?" she responded. "Someone's playing the Hokey Pokey!"

The Crab Soup Eulogy

To understand this story, you have to understand the importance of crabs to the people of Maryland. They are a delicacy, and eating them is a feast that brings family and friends together. My dad was an avid crabber. He would bait crab lines with chicken necks, spending hours in the garage carefully stringing them together the way a musician tunes his guitar.

He had a small, 15-foot boat that he would take out at 2 am to launch on one of the many inlets close to Annapolis. To catch a crab, you had to be on the water at low tide. By around 2 pm, Bess and I would be on alert, watching for his car to pull into the driveway. Dad would always offer a quick thumbs up or thumbs down to describe his catch. Thumbs up meant we would be having a crab feast later in the day, followed by crab cakes later in the week.

My parents often shared crab everything with their friends, Cass and Fred. When I was a little girl, we spent many a New Year's Eve at Cass and Fred's home in Parkville, Maryland or at their place by the beach in Ocean City. Cass was a terrific cook with a vivacious and determined spirit, and she was a good friend to my mom.

When she died, her daughter held a local memorial service for her. All of Cass's friends and family were gathered, solemnly attentive to the priest as he performed the usual duties of respectfully sending her off with fond memories, prayers and love. At one point during the service, he said, "Let's take a moment to bow our heads and pray."

Bess stood up, like an actress given her cue to come on stage, and with a loud rustling of suits and shuffling of shoes, the entire congregation turned to see who on earth was disrupting the solemn prayer.

Bess proceeded to say, "I just wanted to let everyone know that Cass was a wonderful friend, and she made the most delicious crab soup. It was always full of crabmeat and nice vegetables."

The priest quickly reproached her, "Pardon me, but I asked for everyone to bow their heads and pray."

Bess responded, "Oh, I am so terribly sorry, Father, but I thought you said, 'Does anyone have anything to say?'"

The congregation laughed out loud, even Cass's daughter. She still talks about it to this day.

Chapter 17
Lesson Seventeen
Be Prepared to Get Sucked into Your Aging Parents' Off-Kilter Reality

There is no roadmap you can follow to guide you in helping a parent who is getting up there in age. And if your parents are still driving actual cars on literal roads, well, you never know when a mailbox will be taken out or when the men in blue will become more prevalent in their lives. Sometimes, you just won't know what to think about what they are thinking. But if you need a way to get out of getting in trouble, Bess has served up some solid excuses—ahem, reasoning—for her behavior.

On Getting Pulled over by a Cop at 86 Years Old
Returning one day, Bess told me, "I was driving Miss Betty home from our mall visit, and this driver cuts me off and makes me go through a red light."

Uh-oh. "What driver?" I ask.

"The guy on the road," she replies innocently enough.

More uh-oh. "What happened?"

"Well, I see sirens going on, and the police officer pulls me over.

He said, 'Ma'am, do you know you went through a red light?'

And oh, my goodness, he was so cute. He was all dressed up in his police uniform, and he was a doll baby."

"Okay, so what then?"

"Well, I told him like it was. I said, 'Officer, that was not my fault. That man cut me off.'"

"So what did the policeman say?"

"Nothing," Bess beamed. "He smiled and told me to have a nice day and to drive safely. He was as cute as a button. If only I were younger."

(P.S.: I swear this encounter is what started her on her *Cops* television binge.)

Who the F*ck Is Wetchcomb?

As long as I can remember, my mother used a word I've never heard anywhere else in the world. I've asked friends and relatives about it and have even Googled it—nothing. The word is "wetchcomb," and she uses it when she doesn't remember the name of someone she is speaking about.

For example, "Wetchcomb told me that her husband's parents grew up on a farm, and he had to spend every morning milking the cows," or "Wetchcomb told me that her daughter used to do drugs, and I had no idea," or "Wetchcomb had a facelift, and she looks like she just came out of that wax museum from New York City." And then one day, she was telling my brother about someone who died and said, "You know who I mean! She just died. She's Wetchcomb's sister."

Who the f*ck is Wetchcomb, and how would we know her sister?

The Cat Cane

Canes have become a necessary part of Bess's life, and all I can say is that Amazon and canes are a good combo. At times, I feel like I am ordering a new one every month, because Bess leaves them everywhere. One day, my 22-year-old niece, Brooke, noticed that Bess had a new cane, one that none of us had bought for her. As my niece studied it a little more closely, we learned the backstory.

"Bess, where did you get this new cane?" Brooke asked her.

"I got it at the bank."

"No, Bess, I asked you where did you get the cane, the cane?" Brooke asked again.

"I told you, I got it at the bank," Bess insisted.

"What do you mean you got it at the bank?"

"Well, I was in the bank, and one of the bank tellers there gave it to me. Someone left it there. It's a nice cane."

"Do you know there are cats all over it?" Brooke observed.

"Really? Let me see. Oh, I thought they were bugs."

Cut Off a Fingertip? No Problem

One time, Brooke was working a small side job taking care of a pair of Labrador Retrievers. The house where they lived had a very sharp-tipped, wrought iron fence leading into the yard. As she was returning the dogs to their home one night, she opened the gate while juggling the dog's leashes and her pinky finger got caught on one of the spikes, and the tip got sheared off.

I was at Mom's with my sister-in-law when my niece called with the news. Would she lose her fingertip? Would she have to have surgery? She loved to have her nails painted, and all girls want perfect hands to show off their engagement ring one day.

Bess spoke with my niece on the phone the next day and

offered these words of wisdom: "Don't worry about it, Brooke. It'll grow back. "Huh?" I thought. "Is she a lizard?"

The Really, Really Embarrassing Police Story (Holy Sh*t Embarrassing)

I had just brought my mom home from a stint in rehab for a stroke and was driving her car, because I'd traveled to her by train. I parked it in the driveway, came over to the other side of the car to help her get out and walked her into the house. At around 10:30 pm, we put on our pajamas and settled in for the night. I slept with one ear open, as I knew she was still a bit unsteady on her feet. I woke at around 2:30 am to the sound of her footsteps in the kitchen.

"Mom, are you okay?" I yelled out.

"Yes," she said as she shuffled into my bedroom holding the cordless phone to her chest.

"What's wrong?" I asked.

"Well, I don't wanna scare you," Bess explained, "But around 11:30 pm, I heard a lot of noise outside of my window and the sound of a bunch of kids running. I looked out the window, and since that time, there's been a strange car parked in my driveway."

"What do you mean? What did you hear?" I rubbed my eyes until my sleep-blurry vision turned clear.

"I heard a lot of noise and rustling around the windows, and I think someone ran away from the car. Look how dark that car is and how long it is. Isn't that a long car? I don't know anybody who has a car as long as that. It's ugly."

"I don't know, Ma. Are you sure it's not Bud's car or one of his kids' cars? Let's think. It isn't mine. Whose car could it be?"

"I don't know," replied Bess, "but there's been an awful lot of break-ins around here lately, and it may be some nut out there."

"Okay, Mom. Let's not turn the lights on." As I squatted beneath the windowsill, peering outside, my heart started pounding. Was someone casing out the house, knowing that an elderly woman lived there by herself? Finally, I couldn't take it anymore.

"I'm calling 911," I said.

"Hee!" Bess responded.

"What's wrong with you? Shhh," I told her. "I'm on the phone."

"You're so funny. You are so serious."

"Ma, be quiet. I don't want anyone to hear us or the guy in the car outside to see us."

The friendly woman dispatcher said it was best to keep quiet; we shouldn't look out the windows and we had to stay together.

In about a minute, we saw flashing lights on the street as two
Bel Air police officers positioned their patrol cars to shine their
lights on our suspected intruder's long, dark sedan. The police
officer walked around the car, flashing his light inside.

Deliberately, he walked back to his patrol car, turned on his
inside car light and wrote something down on his official
docket. My mom and I huddled in the darkness awaiting his
findings, like how you'd wait to open the envelope containing
your report card in grade school. Finally, he approached the
front door. We slowly opened it. Our hair was disheveled, and
we both had reading glasses on. We were a full-blown, dreadful
sight.

"Good evening, Ma'am," greeted the police officer.

"Oh officer, we are so worried," Bess said. "You know there've
been a lot of break-ins around here lately."

"Ma'am, do you own a 2011 Toyota Corolla?" the officer asked.

"Why yes, officer, I do."

"Well, that's your car," the officer responded.

Holy sh*t. I quickly realized what had happened. Bess always,
and I mean always, parks her car in the garage. For as long as
she has lived in her home, that car never spent a single night
outside. Until that one. Beyond mortified, I thanked the police
officer profusely, quickly closed the door and headed upstairs

in anticipation of burying myself under the covers as deeply as I could. Meanwhile, Bess was downstairs laughing her ass off.

"I haven't had a good laugh like that since I can't remember when," she chuckled.

"Ma, you must promise me you will never tell anyone about tonight," I told her. "I feel ridiculous."

After a few minutes, we settled into bed, me in one room and my mother in the next. Every three seconds, she'd burst out laughing. I, on the other hand, couldn't believe that I had been sucked into her web of insanity and actually believed her fears about the car! I'd totally forgotten that I had parked it there when we came home. I was just as asinine as she was.

"I bet this will be in *The Aegis*," Bess called to me. "They always put these kinds of things in the newspaper. I bet you they'll say a police officer was called to my address for a suspicious car, but instead, it was some nut and her daughter who reported a suspicious car that was theirs!"

That about summed it up, all right.

Chapter 18
Lesson Eighteen
Overdose on Endorphins and Dopamine with the Chemistry of Laughter

Humor helps everyone keep their sanity, especially when dealing with issues of aging. Sometimes I can't tell if Bess is being funny on purpose or by accident, but it doesn't really matter because she keeps us all laughing.

Dead Batteries Daily

In her mid-80s, Mom started to have this little problem where she just couldn't remember to turn the light switch off in her car. Most of the time, she'd hit it by accident, but the result was near-daily instances of a dead car battery. My brother would get random calls from her while she was out shopping with her girlfriend, and he would have to meet her in the middle of the mall parking lot to jumpstart the car. We finally decided it was time to get her AAA.

Thankfully, the random calls stopped, but the dead batteries didn't; in fact, one weekend, I came to visit and learned she had made a new friend to help with her dead battery issues. I went into her garage to start up the car, and guess what? Dead. The car was parked nose-in, so I had no idea how we were going to jumpstart it.

"Mom, I just tried to start your car, and your battery is dead."

"Okay," Bess replied, "I can call the man."

"What man?"

"The dead battery man," she repeated.

"The car is in the garage facing the wall. How is he going to jumpstart it? We are going to have to push it out of the garage."

"No, we don't. They have a long cord they hook to the battery from their car."

"How do you know?" I asked.

"The man comes here all the time. He probably knows me by name."

"What's his name?"

"I have no idea, but he's as nice as he can be."

On Dry Lips
"My lips are so dry," I told Bess.

"Go get some of my Vaseline in the cabinet," she answered.

"You know, Mom, I've noticed that Vaseline in there for a very, very long time. How old is it?"

"Gosh, your dad brought that home when your brother was a baby."

My brother is 63 years old—that sh*t wasn't going on my lips!

On Wearing Thongs

During a visit to Bess's neurologist, she and I were sitting in a waiting room full of 20 patients, most of them middle-aged. Some were quietly reading, one was watching the television and others were surfing the web on their smartphones. Bess, as she always does, was evaluating the attire of the woman sitting across from us. I watched her eyes flick from the woman's head to her toes, and she suddenly pointed at her and blurted out for all to hear, "I used to wear thongs. I don't wear them anymore, though. I used to love my thongs."

Every single person in that waiting room looked up and turned toward my mother. I paused for a few seconds and said, "Bess, you mean flip-flops, right?"

"Well, of course I do," she replied. "What did you think I meant?"

The woman sitting across from us said, "Thong underwear!"

Bess laughed so hard she was gasping. "Are you crazy?" she chortled, trying to catch her breath. "I didn't mean that.

Besides, I don't know how people wear those things anyway. They're a pain in the ass."

Literally.

On Big Baseball Salaries

"Did you hear about Mammy Machiatto and all that money he is making?" Bess asked me.

"Who?"

"That Mammy guy, the football player."

"Do you mean Manny Machado, the baseball player for the San Diego Padres who signed a contract for $300 million?"

"Yes, Mammy Machiatto."

On My Nephew Watching Ass Surgeries

In one of Holly and Bess's conversations, my daughter asked about the new job her cousin, who was Bess's grandson, got working for a medical supply company that sold surgical mesh for hernia surgeries.

"Bess, I heard Justin got a new job. Does he like it?"

"He loves it," Bess told her. "He gets to wear surgical scrubs. He sells stuff for hemorrhoids and watches hemorrhoid surgeries."

"What? He's doing what?"

"He watches hemorrhoid surgeries all day long."

Hernia and hemorrhoids—almost the same thing?

On the 11 O'Clock News
"It's time to watch the news. I want to see who got shot."

On Getting High-Definition TV
"Everyone looks skinnier now. They used to be fat. The one woman with big hips looks normal now. Maybe the weather-girl's arms will be shorter now, too."

On the Smell of Fajitas in Our Favorite Restaurant
"Those chaquitas smell so good when they come out."

On Being Asked If She Wanted Any Dip from the Supermarket
"I thought you said do I want any dick, and I don't need any of that."

On Sleeping in until 1:30 pm
"I was up until midnight watching *Cops*. They put the juicy stuff in the later shows."

In the Movie Theater, Loudly for All to Hear, During *A Star is Born*

"I could make love to Bradley Cooper anytime."

On the Town Acquaintance Whose Pet Spider Monkey Got Caught Pleasuring Itself in Front of a Nun

"Oh, that's normal. The poor thing has no toys to play with all day, so it has to find something to play with."

On God's Mistakes

"Next time, I hope the Lord does a better job and brings us women back without periods."

On Being Happy

"I can't say I'm dis-happy. Wait, is that even a word?"

On the Medical Alert Commercial Where the Lady is on the Floor and Can't Get Up

"That young medic can come help me get up anytime. Isn't he cute? But that woman lying on the floor, don't you hate her? She gets on my nerves."

On the Attorney Commercial for Injury Compensation

"How come I can't get compensation for my injuries?" Bess asked.

"What injuries?" I replied, puzzled.

"My back, my old bones, my bad legs."

"Did someone cause those injuries?"

"Oh, does someone have to cause injuries for you to get compensation?"

On Her Thin Pal
"I saw my friend I haven't seen for a while, and she was as skinny as an electric cord."

On Her Friend's Driving
"She won't make left turns or go backward, so it takes her a while to get to places."

On My Husband Golfing at the Country Club
"Let me pack him a sandwich and put it in a brown bag. He may get hungry out there all that time."

On World-Class Ocean-Front Resorts
"Ocean City, Maryland, has the best ocean-front beaches in the world. I was disappointed in Las Vegas beaches." (FYI: Las Vegas is land-locked.)

On the Long Wait at the Red Light
"This light is so long you could bake a cake."

The Many Ways Bess Misremembers the Name of Alice, Our Cleaning Lady
"Lola does a good job."

"Ella is so sweet."

"Stella is late today."

On Her Friend Who Fell in Church and Broke a Hip
"I think Jesus may have tripped her because he was so surprised to see her."

On Me Covering Her in Bed at Night With Her Comforter When She Gets Cold
"My girlfriend used to tell her husband, 'Just cover me up when you're done.'"

On Offspring from Good-Looking People
"My friend is so pretty, but Christ, her kid is ugly. I don't understand that."

On the Importance of a Strategic Beach Location
"When my friends and I would go to the beach when I was a little younger, we'd look to find the fattest people we could and then sit next to them so we'd look skinny."

On Being Summoned for Jury Duty
"I sent them a little note on a piece of paper and told them I won't be able to make it."

On Losing Her Memory
"Mom, be easy on yourself. Remember, you have a little dementia," Bud tried to assure Bess.

"I do? Oh, I forgot about that."

Chapter 19
Lesson Nineteen
Try Not to Fight That Which You Can't Control

W hen I was little, my mother told me to run the water when I peed. This created problems. I ended up with bashful kidneys, which was a pain in the ass in college and in public restrooms in general, or any time I had to pee within earshot of someone. Why did we have to run the water every time we went to the bathroom so no one would hear us? According to Bess, "That's just the way it was back then."

Over the years, pee has become a fun ongoing topic. Besides the fear of hearing pee, I remember my mother sometimes laughing so hard she would pee her pants. Bess will tell you this is much more common than you think.

On How Everyone Pees Their Pants
Every one of us dreads the moment when packages of Depend-brand underwear become as much of a house staple as peanut butter. In fact, I do Kegel exercises daily to try and thwart the

eventual possibility of adult diapers. Still, I'm curious what it's like to wear them, so one day, I asked Bess.

"They're like wearing a wet diaper," she explained. "We used to have to worry about sanitary napkins, and now, you have to worry about Depends. They cheat you, too. They usually give you six in a pack, and sometimes, they act like they are giving you 12 extra Depends in some of their bonus packs, but I think they're taking the lining out and putting it in the other six. It's a scam."

One day, she accidentally bought the men's version. You can tell the difference because the men's style have a little flap in the front. I found out later that night she tried to pawn them off on my brother. He doesn't wear them, but according to my mother, everyone should. Really, Bess should be a brand ambassador.

"I just got home from a work trip, Mom," I told her over the phone one day. "How are you?"

"I'm fine." Bess responded. "Where were you?"

"In Florida. The terminal at JFK is so long and I was rushing. I had to go to the bathroom so bad. I'm just so happy to be home."

"You should wear Depends when you travel! You'd never have to stop to go to the bathroom. It's wonderful."

"Bess, are you high? I'm not wearing Depends."

"Well, you should. Everybody should. Everyone pees their pants, and if they tell you they don't, they're lying."

A few years later, we all visited Mom for Easter, and my daughter took the train down from Connecticut, where she was attending college. My brother's family and mine were out having a night of fun at a local restaurant with Bess when Holly popped out of her chair to go to the ladies' room.

"Where is Holly going?" Bess asked.

"She's going to the bathroom," I replied.

As Holly walked away, Bess pointed her finger at her and said, her voice echoing loudly, "She should wear Depends, too."

On the Diaper Bag
"Christ, I feel like I'm carrying a diaper bag when I am out—I have snacks, a sweater, hard candy and Depends."

On Delicately Checking How Her Undergarments Are Doing
"Are you wet?" I inquire.

"Why, is it raining?" she asks.

On Identifying a Leak
Sometimes, a pair of Depends just doesn't work. Luckily, our sense of humor always seems to.

On one of my visits home, Bud, Bess and I decided to try a new pizza restaurant. Bess loves her pizza, so instead of going for the $10 ultra-thin crust special at the chain a few doors down, we checked out the hip, new spot, the one with slatted wooden chairs and a bit of a metro feel.

About halfway through the meal, I noticed what appeared to be some sort of a puddle underneath her chair. My brother and I looked above to see if there was any sort of a leak. We looked down at the floor to see if someone spilled a soda and then we looked at Bess, and together, we started to laugh. I cleaned up the puddle, despite the waitress wanting to assist. Needless to say, we have not returned. Her Depends were undependable that night.

Chapter 20
Lesson Twenty
You Have to Dig Deep When Things Get Bad—and You Will

Okay, so there are books to help when you are expecting a child but not much out there to prepare you for your parents getting old. To be fair, this may be because it isn't fun, and yes, I never in my entire life anticipated sitting on the floor with my brother, putting my mom's underwear on her while he held her up. Dressing your parent is not something one ever expects, but it is a real scenario, and this (or some variation) will probably happen to most people.

The underwear incident was like the time after one of Bess's strokes, when she was slowly getting back to herself but not completely, and the three of us were doing the best we could. Bess was shooting out words and sentences that fell into certain categories but that weren't making sense. It was like her brain's filing cabinet had emptied onto the floor and the folders had gotten mixed up. The phenomenon has a name: aphasia.

She would say things like, "Put the pickle in the toaster," and she would get frustrated because she meant something more like, "Put the orange juice in the refrigerator," or, "Hand me my eye makeup box." Mom knew what she was saying wasn't making sense, but after a dozen or so of these offerings, we just started cracking up, Bess included. It was a laugh of love and unity, a sort of relief during a stressful, crazy time.

Once, we thought Bess was having a third small stroke, but she ended up being diagnosed with the flu and dehydration. She wasn't making sense, so they suspected a stroke was affecting her word retrieval, causing aphasia again, but I understood her completely. Speaking with her over the phone while she was in the hospital was like an exercise from my Spanish translation class.

"Hi, Robin. I'm doing okay," she told me (Robin is my sister-in-law). "The ice cream is great, and it is taking good care of me. Oh, your scrags still look really nice." By "ice cream" she meant "hospital," and by "scrags" she was referring to the flowers I sent her for Christmas. "Go home and take care of the children," Bess continued. "Don't drive down from New York, Sis." Sis was what she always called her older sister, who passed away a few years ago.

She has always told us she would be fine if anything happened because she would push her medical alert button, which has become its own irony. That thing has been a godsend for us in detecting her falls; however, whenever she has an episode, she instead screams out the window, and of course, in the dead of winter, nobody hears her.

"I am so mad no one came," she said. "They should have heard me."

"Mom, why didn't you just push the button? That's why it's there!"

Bess responded after a long pause, "Hmm. Ya know, I never thought of that. That's dumb, isn't it?"

I'm glad to be able to help my mother, but being helpful sometimes feels quite a lot like being helpless. Some of the moments in these latter years of my mother's life have been quite poignant, and I will treasure them—like the time my brother and I gave her a shower when she was in the hospital. She looked up at us, no teeth and no modesty, the most vulnerable a human being could be. It is so hard to see your own mother that way.

Yes, we knew bathing was the ultimate feel-good formula; she'd taught us that, so we were trying to give it back to her as a sort of remedy, a token of our love. It was like trying to put someone back together again. Later that day, she turned to me and said, "You are the best thing that ever happened to me. Do you think Holly will take care of you the way you and Buddy take care of me? You are doing just like I did with my mother."

But not everyone sees our caretaking like Bess does, especially those viewing from a distance. But people who aren't living what you're living can easily provide their thoughts and opinions. They can be quick to judge from the outside, thinking you should be making different choices, but ultimately, only you know what steps you need to do what works best for you, your family and your loved ones. The bottom line is this: the only things you want for your parents as they age are to be safe and comfortable, and to protect their dignity. That is truly what matters.

I don't always know if I'm achieving that goal, but there was once a moment that I believe an angel from heaven sent me a message that I needed.

I had come down from New York for a few days during a holiday weekend, and within the first 24 hours, I had gotten a five-foot snake removed from Bess's deck that had eaten all the baby birds in her bird "whorehouse," spent an hour on the phone resolving a delinquent hospital payment and stumbled upon some leaking pipes with no plumbers available to fix them. I was spent. However, I was still determined to get Bess and myself to her beloved nail place for a much-needed, mid-pandemic day out—for both of us.

After our nails were finished, we went out for dinner. In the restaurant parking lot, trying to get her out of the car was comical. In the few months prior, she had developed this strange tick that only Bess would have of loudly laughing for no reason. This was not a quiet laugh, mind you, but a head-turning, what's-so-funny-I-want-to-hear-the-joke-too laugh. It annoyed Bess so much that every few times it occurred, she'd even yell at herself, "Shut up!" It got to a point where I would ask, "Are you laughing, or is that the thing again?"

On this particular day, I didn't have time to ask. When I opened the car door, her laughing shriek rose to a level that scared the sh*t out of me. I jumped and screamed from her scream, and then we just cracked up together. We laughed and struggled at the same time. Our toes were still tacky from the pedicure as I slowly put her shoes back on and got her walker. We shuffled our way into the restaurant, stopping for Bess to take a break along the way.

As we slowly proceeded to our table, an older woman came from behind and tapped me on the shoulder.

"I want to congratulate you on how you are taking care of your mother," she said. "I watched you get her out of the car, help her with her shoes and walker and bring her in patiently. Not everyone treats their parents like that, and it is wonderful to see. God bless you. She is so lucky to have you." That day, at least for that moment, I felt like my brother and I were truly achieving our goal.

Any day can be a struggle. It goes like this: Today, Mom had a good day. The next day: Mom had a bad day. In other words, at a certain age, life is day by day, and it takes a lot of support to get through each one. People say it takes a community to raise a child; it takes one to fight for your parent's safety, comfort and dignity as they age as well.

Bess celebrating her 90 years of wisdom

Bess and I at a family wedding in 2020

*Bess and our family returning to New York City for a fun,
family weekend in 2017*

Chapter 21
Lesson Twenty-One
It Is Not Natural to Tell Your Mom to Eat Her Peas, but One Day, You Will Have To—and Then Some

We learn from our parents and call on them for guidance throughout our lives, but there comes a day when you switch roles. You step in because they can no longer see clearly, judge wisely, or because they are just too darn stubborn to realize they have to take a step back. When you try to make sure they eat their vegetables and take their vitamins, or when you put up big signs to remind them to *turn off the iron*, two things come to mind: you will call on those same lessons and guidance they taught you to get you through it, and you'll forget what it was like when they were in the driver's seat, literally and figuratively. If you are lucky, like me, you will also get some big laughs along the way.

Letting Go of the Car

The thought of your child driving when they turn 16 is beyond scary. The thought of your 87-year-old mother driving could possibly be worse.

The most difficult part of having the discussion about not driving anymore is the fact that you are single-handedly taking away their independence. Trying to get Bess to give up her car was like a tug of war between two gorillas. Every week, Bud and I noticed some new scratches and dents; then, we'd get the secondhand story of Bess taking out a mailbox or two. Finally, she relented—well, I did have to massage the truth a bit.

I told her my daughter needed a car and that her 10-year-old Toyota Corolla, with its gentle 17,000 miles of usage on side roads, would be perfect. That seemed to be the magic message. Suddenly, Bess felt she was helping us. To her, she was not saying she could no longer drive. Instead, she was supporting her granddaughter and passing on one of her most prized possessions. We bought the car for my daughter, but that wasn't the end of the discussion.

"I know I don't have my car anymore, and I hate it. Can I drive someone else's car?" Bess kept asking.

A few months later, she said, "I'm glad I gave up my car. Besides, I would drive and forget where I was at."

"Mom, you never told me that!" I was only semi-shocked.

"Well, it was just a few times."

To this day, Bess asks me how her car is running. She tells me how she misses it and even asks me every now and then if I would sell it back to her.

"Okay. Do you think you'll use it?" I ask to call her bluff.

She pauses and says, "Nah, you keep it. I can't drive it anymore."

Rocketman, Tinman and Lights Out

The year that the Elton John biopic *Rocketman* was in theaters, we made a date to see it, figuring the time period and music from the '60s and '70s would be familiar to both Bess and her friend Betty. These days, it literally takes my mother three hours before any event to get ready, so we were running a bit late after picking up Miss Betty. *No problem*, I thought. *Those damn previews play for half an hour anyhow.* But this day, they did not.

I entered the theater with Betty on my left arm and Bess on my right, both of them walking with hesitant strides as they struggled to adjust to the darkness and loudness. When we finished inching down the ramp that led to the seats, we were in front of dozens of people waiting for the show to start.

My mom's hearing loss tends to make her speak even louder than she used to. The screen flashed long enough to allow us to see the audience, and Bess said, "Look, there are people here!" The crowd chuckled.

And then, before I could find us three open seats together, the previews were over and the lights went black—and I mean, we weren't seeing anything. In my head, I panicked. *I didn't see this one coming*, I thought. *I didn't plan for this. What do I do now?*

Like tiny mice coming face-to-face with an alley cat, Betty and Bess froze. I couldn't pull, push or cajole them into moving.

"I can't see!" Miss Betty announced. "Are there steps here? Where are we?"

Even louder, Bess exclaimed, "I don't know where we are. Where are the seats?"

"Ma," I said, "trust me. Take my hand and walk behind me. I've got you."

Seconds in this limbo seemed like hours.

"Where is the seat?" they kept asking. "Where are the steps? We can sit right here." Back and forth they went like dueling banjos, tugging on my arms like I was their escort through a haunted house. Suddenly, Bess adamantly declared, "I am not moving until the lights come back on!"

"Well, that's a problem," I chirped, "as the lights won't be coming on for at least two hours. We have to make a move."

I pleaded with them to trust me and just walk slowly to the neck-twisting seats by the screen, the ones that are usually only available when the movie sells out. By that point, I would've sat on the floor if I could have.

"Where's the usher with the flashlight?" Bess boomed. I had never used an usher in my life, and I don't think they even exist anymore, but one sure would have come in handy. Finally, I was able to get them into their seats, which sparked another barrage of questions: "Where are we? Did the movie start? Why are we sitting here?"

Like a mom settling in toddlers, I passed them their smuggled Diet Cokes with straws, a bag of cashews, some popcorn and a small bag of Hershey's samplers.

Still, my mother shouted, "Miss Betty doesn't have her drink. Where is her drink? Didn't you bring her one?"

"Mom," I replied, "you're drinking her drink. You have the other one in your hand."

They both giggled, and Bess continued to talk loudly, seeking answers from Miss Betty about what was happening in the movie and laughing even louder at every costume Elton John wore. I finally said, "Ma, you must be quiet. People are trying to watch the movie."

"You're no fun," she quipped. "Why are you always so serious?"

A few minutes later, Betty moved toward Bess's ear and asked, "What's going on? What is that man doing to the other man?"

"I think he's giving him a bl*wj*b," Bess asserted with gusto.

She was right. She can't see and can't hear, but she got that one spot on.

A little bit later, after the movie was over, my mom declared: "I liked *Tinman*, but it was a little deep." I didn't bother correcting her that the movie was called *Rocketman*.

On DNA and Ancestral Resemblance

Growing up, I always asked my parents what our heritage was. Every time I asked, I got a different answer because they only knew what their parents had told them, and those stories were inconsistent.

On the phone one time, I reminded my mom that we knew what our heritage was because I had done some DNA tests and had researched our lineage. She said that she'd forgotten what we were, and I explained that we were primarily English with some other European influences. I reminded her how that was quite fascinating, as our lineage indicated that we also had ancestors in Mongolia. It was a very small percentage, but it was interesting nonetheless.

"Really?" Bess accepted this news and weighed in with her own opinions. "I've always tanned well, and the closer I get to turning 90, I'm starting to look Mongolian."

Friday Night Is Not the Time to Talk Funerals

Mom has made it clear that she has one steadfast rule for her funeral, and that is to make sure her hair is perfect—not like my dad's.

"Make sure Millie does my hair. I already talked to her about it," she has told me more than once. "Also, I want to be laid out in the dress I wore at your wedding. Although, who is even going to come? They're all dead."

Mom thinks about this often, and every now and then, I get the "I want to talk to you about something" conversation starter. Like the winter evening after dinner, in the middle of biting into one of her beloved Kit Kat bars (thank goodness the President didn't ban them), when she familiarly began, "Now, I want to talk about what to lay me out in when I die."

"Okay, that again?" I respond.

"You know, I think you can put me in the pink dress from your wedding that I wore," she continued, "or maybe that other outfit, that white suit."

"Okay," I said, "But Mom, that pink dress is 30 years old. I think it will be too big on you now."

She looked at me wide-eyed and paused before emphatically stating, "Well, that's no problem; they just pin it all up to make it fit when you're dead."

"Okay, got it," I acknowledged, then quickly retorted, "Wait, what about that white suit you mentioned? Maybe that would be better."

"That depends," Bess replied stoically.

"On what?"

"The weather."

"The weather?" I asked, perplexed.

"Yeah," she went on, "If I die in the summer, I'm not wearing that heavy suit because it's too damn hot. I'll be uncomfortable."

Then, there was the Friday night I called her to catch up on my drive home from work.

"Listen, we need to talk about my funeral," Bess told me.

"Okay, Mom. That's fine, and I'll be down next week. We can talk then. I don't want to talk about it this very moment as it is 5:30 on a Friday night, and the conversation is just a little bit too heavy for me."

So Bess asked me, "What? My funeral is goin' to be at 5:30 on Friday night?"

The Little Black Pill

Referring to herself, Bess says, "If I fall down the steps, just give me the little black pill."

Referring to someone else in worse shape than her, she says, "If I ever get like that, just give me the little black pill."

"Mom, can you let me know where this little black pill is, and can you save one for me?" is my response.

On Me Bringing Her Dinner to Her in Front of the TV
"You'd make a cute waitress!"

On the $11,000 She Had Left in the Bank
"Do you think that $33 million will last me?"

On Losing Items in Her Sleep
"When I was young and married, I used to wake up scared and search for my wedding ring in the sheets when I lost it in the bed at night. Now I wake up in a panic to try to find my bottom teeth."

The Disappearing Phones
Bess and phones are like the mystery of socks in the dryer: two socks go in, but somehow, only one comes out. We have four cordless phones in her house at any given time: one in the bedroom, one in her TV room, one in the kitchen and one in the basement. Most of the time, they resurface. Other times, well, they get buried a little bit.

On one of those latter times, Bess asked, "Did you try to call me today?"

"Not before now," I replied.

"Oh. The phone rang like 30 times. I couldn't find it because I was sitting on it."

During another visit on our way home from a restaurant, Bess asked, "When we get home, I need to look for my phones. I can't find any of my phones. I've been missing them since two days ago."

"Mom, how can you keep losing your phones? It doesn't make sense."

"I know," she responded. "Hand me my purse. I want to get my lipstick out."

I handed her the overstuffed bag. Rummaging through, Bess said, "Gosh, I need to clean out my purse. There's so much junk in here. Bon, here, hold this phone while I look for the lipstick."

Phones in Strange Places

Four phones. Dead phones. No phones. Phones ringing from beyond. One day, our entire family was calling Bess, and she was not answering. It was because she had misplaced all four of her cordless phones. It was like a game of Clue as we tried to retrace each of the phones' journeys. In fact, I think we even poked our heads in the dryer to see if they somehow found their way into the laundry cycle. Eventually, we found three of the phones. Then on the day the aide came, I received this text:

I found the other phone this morning when I was putting away her laundry. It was in the underwear drawer.

Movie Night

Growing up, you couldn't drag my mom to a movie.

"I'm not going to any damn movie!" she would say. "I'll pull my hair out. I want to go somewhere where I can dance and meet people." Now, she likes movies—she even likes the documentaries. We watch both a lot, but she doesn't remember them after she watches them, so I keep a mental note of the ones she liked the best, so she can watch them again.

When I put a movie on, Bess always asks, "Am I going to like this?"

Each time, I can convincingly say, "Yes, you absolutely will. I am 100 percent sure."

One day, tired of the movies we were rewatching, I offered her documentaries on Netflix. She was amazed.

"How come I never knew I got this channel?" she asked. "What does this cost?" There were three choices for biopics: Frank Sinatra, Betty White or Jackie O. Frank Sinatra it was, and oh, how she loved that Frank's wife, Nancy, was a good housekeeper.

"Everyone should be like that," she said. Then, in the middle of a verse of Frank singing "I've Got You Under My Skin," she turned to me and assertively asked, "Is he dead yet?"

These days, aside from my selection of the repeat movies I know she'll like, the only other thing I feel 100 percent certain of is that there is nothing that prepares you for the hard decisions that await each and every one of us when it comes to our moms and dads. Caring for a parent does, however, test your fortitude, empathy, integrity and patience (and at least 20 other qualities).

Through it all, I can't help but remember the mom I grew up with, and I try desperately to recall what interacting with her was like when she was in charge. Those familiar and reliable daily interactions disappear and shift into something odd and uncomfortable. As a result, if you're like me, you try to hold onto their essence—the lessons.

Chapter 22
Lesson Twenty-Two: The Final Lesson
Your Mom Is Your Anchor, Your Lens through Which Life Evolves

I've had a lot of interesting conversations with my mom recently. Although her memory is compromised, her best and worst memories have surfaced to the top of her mind like robust foam on a savored cappuccino.

Interestingly, I don't recall many bad childhood memories, but there is one from when I was about seven that I remember vividly. I used to love helping my mom bake our annual sugar cookies three weeks before Christmas. It was the official launch of the Christmas countdown. She would make the dough a few days ahead of time, as it had to be the right texture for optimal baking.

I recall the floury feel of the rolling pin cloth, the sound of the oven door slamming after each dozen was placed inside and the occasional burned smell of the cookies we would purposely bake well-done for our neighbor, Mr. Lawrence, who loved them crunchy and brown. The baking event was an all-day affair.

My job was to sprinkle the cookies with cinnamon and sugar, and I took it very seriously. One year, we even made cupcakes, and my job was to sprinkle the jimmies. For us, jimmies weren't the oblong chocolate candy toppings, but rather those small and spherical multicolored sugar balls.

That year, as an excited, fast-moving seven-year-old with an abundance of Christmas spirit, I sang "Jingle Bells" as I sprinkled—but I forgot the jimmies were to the right of my sprinkle hand, which I flourished dramatically as I hit the high note, spraying the candies all over the tiny kitchen floor. I could hear them racing by the hundreds along the laminated strip like rain on a window, pinging under the stove and refrigerator.

Bess lost her mind. There was no Roomba to come to the rescue back then, and she was overwhelmed at the thought of chasing down those ant-attracting sugar balls. She was probably PMS-ing or had had a long day, but all I remember was the sound of her screaming, "G*dd*mmit!"

I took off running and crying, knowing, as I hyperventilated, that I would be scarred by the moment for the rest of my life. We never talked about that event after. And then, while she and I were having one of our many conversations, Bess, at 88, said out of the blue: "I should have never yelled at you for knocking over those jimmies. I'm sorry."

Now, Bess rarely says she is sorry, and I was blown away; first, that she would even remember that day some half a century ago, and second, that she would apologize for it. But in a strange way, I'm so happy she did. It was a connection—a good one. We laughed, and I told her how the seven-year-old me had felt about it but assured her that I was quite fine. It's funny, the things that stick. In this case, jimmies.

Some details of life have inexplicably fallen away. My mom doesn't remember my birthday anymore. We were visiting Brenda's Beauty Boutique, going down the aged, concrete steps for her hair appointment, when she asked me what day it was.

"It's December 7th," I said.

"Oh, Pearl Harbor Day," she responded. Then she paused and said, "I think that's someone's birthday."

"Yep, it's mine!" I said.

"Aww, how old are you now?" Mom asked.

"I'm 55."

To which she said sweetly, "Are you that old now?"

It was like she was talking to a fond acquaintance.

Your mom is the one who makes you feel like your birthday is the most important day in the world. She hugs you first thing in the morning and plants a red lipstick-ed smack on your little cheek. She's the first one to sing to you as a toddler, she brings you McDonald's in grade school and she's the first one who calls to congratulate you on getting another year older when you're away at college. Things like that no longer happen between Bess and me, but it doesn't really matter. I know the love is still the same in her heart, and the memories and experiences of birthday love from my childhood make it all okay.

Before I blew out the candles on the many birthday cakes she made me over the years, Bess would always tell me, "You can do anything you put your mind to. Make a wish." When I was little, I liked when she said that. It gave me a sense of determination. Her words made me feel like I had a secret key, a potion that no one else had. It made me feel unique. Someone believed in me.

Over the years, I've asked Bess what she would have been if

she'd had the encouragement and opportunity to go to school like I did. She always answered the same way.

"I would've liked to be a nurse. Something in the medical field," she would say. Then, she'd add, "I have no regrets. I've had a great life—a good husband, good kids, a nice home and some great parties with wonderful friends. I don't need a whole lot. I just like to take care of the little bit that I do have."

Bess helped me see how big that little bit can be. When I was a little girl, my family didn't have a lot, but we had more than enough, for sure. At around 10 years old, I swam on our community swim team. I wasn't very good, but I hung in there because my pals were on the team too.

God, how I hated that ice-cold water during the 8 am practices! Our team was from Baltimore, and once a season, we would travel 45 minutes north to compete in Fallston, where the "rich and snobby" people lived. At that time and place in my life, the people there had nicer cars, bigger homes and a better, private swim club pool to compete in. It turned out they weren't snobby, but rather middle-class folks who had more than we did. They weren't rich by any means.

Ironically, a few years later, we moved to the town nearby in a modest home, moving up in the world. I know for certain, as it became apparent to me during many of our conversations years later, that Bess felt that the move contributed to a different teenage experience for me. Was it better? I believe it was. Why? Because it provided me with the absolute best high school experience I could have dreamed of—John Carroll School in Bel Air, Maryland—with friends I still cherish today, even if the transition wasn't easy at first.

Changing schools was a hard adjustment. I went from a small, conservative Catholic school in Baltimore to a larger public school where fights broke out weekly between kids in the hall and the cool kids drank on the weekends and smoked in the school bathrooms. But I had an eighth-grade teacher who took an interest in me and my writing. His name was Mr. Helmkemp. In fact, I still have the end-of-year comments he wrote on my report card in 1979. He said, "Bonnie has a special talent for writing, and I hope she continues to develop it."

I must have read those words 20 times over the next few years, and I still have that report card today, saved in my important stuff folder, housed between Social Security cards, vaccinations, passports and birth certificates. I'd like to send him this book, along with those comments made 40-some years ago to say thank you. That early shot of confidence from having someone I looked up to believing I was good at something and making my mom and dad proud has fueled many a journey through my professional years. But it makes my heart also feel a little sad for Bess. I wish she'd had a Mr. Helmkemp or a parent to encourage her to follow her dreams when she was young. She would have made a fine nurse. So, I thank my mom for believing in me.

Over the years, I've interviewed my mom with my ear bent on collecting her unique words, her wit and wisdom. I always gave her little updates on how the work was coming along. When she was ailing or having a health issue, I thought talking about the book would give her a lift and make her feel special. I think it did. Whether we were out and about, meeting someone new or just keeping an appointment with Millie the hairdresser, she'd often say proudly, pointing to me as she spoke, "You know, she's writing a book about me." The person she told would just smile and nod, most likely thinking, *Okay, lady.*

Although she never had a Mr. Helmkemp, I hope she knows she has something even better. She has someone who thinks she's special enough to write a book about.

Every time we talked about something new, and I told her I was going to add it to a section, or when I would say, "Wait, I have to write that down—that's going in the book," she'd laugh.

"You think I'm funny?" she'd say. "Everyone used to tell me I was funny. My girlfriends always said, 'Bess, you're so funny.' I never thought I was," and she'd roll her eyes. "But I guess I'm funny."

And it is fun and quite funny, this world according to Bess.

"I hope you make a lot of money on this damn book," she told me sarcastically one day. When I told her that was a long shot, and I was just hoping to get it published, she said, "Why are you doing this, then? Why are you spending so much time on this? It's so much work."

Wow was my unspoken response. I hadn't really thought about things in those terms. I knew writing a book about my mother was something I wanted to do, but why I was so compelled to do it wasn't something I'd consciously thought about. It didn't take long for me to realize the reasons. I haven't shared them with her, but I am sharing them here, because it all comes full circle.

The first reason I wrote this book is because I can't think of anything more special than to pay tribute to the person in my life who has had the single, greatest impact on shaping who I've become. Your mom is the first one to hold you, soothe you and welcome you into this world, and if you're lucky, you will be the last one they see before they leave this earth.

The second reason is that I believe my mom's generation has a lot of good insight and wisdom. Through her experiences, I see what we've lost with our focus on immediacy and technology. We've progressed in countless ways but have sacrificed in others, like face-to-face communication and connecting with our families and each other. She got that right. Relationships are so critical to life.

The third reason is because watching Bess age has been a challenge for my family, and detailing it in these pages has truly been a cathartic and therapeutic exercise that I'm hoping will help others who are in this same place. I'm a bit blown away by just how hard the aging process is. Everyone wants to live a relevant and independent life, and there's not enough societal support for the aging folks among us who deserve it. It is our responsibility as their children to try to protect that right and dignity.

Fourth, I've always aspired to and dreamt of one day writing a book. I used to create my own books as a little girl, cutting up construction paper, using colored pencils for the text and staples for the binding. Being an author has always been on the ol' bucket list, but it was a dream I rarely shared because I had no idea what I would write about. My experiences with Bess and my compulsion to tell her story have given me the motivation.

This brings me to the fifth and final reason. As Bess told me over and over throughout my childhood, if you put your mind to it, you really and truly and absolutely can do most anything at all. She is right, and this book is proof. Of all the funny things and sage advice Bess has shared with me over the years, the one thing that has stayed with me the most powerfully is her motto: *"Yes, You can!"*

Now, go hug your mother!

Me presenting my mom with the final manuscript of the book

Acknowledgments

It Takes a Village to Raise a Child, to Care For an Aging Parent and to Encourage You to Write a Book

I have many people to thank for giving me the courage to bring my mother's personality and perspective to life. Of course, I am grateful to my husband John and daughter Holly, my life's greatest gift and blessing, who give me the motivation every day to work hard to be the best person I can be. I know I can be a bit intense, but for the most part, it is driven by love. I only hope my mother's belief in me and her recognition of the importance of empowering yourself through education and hard work is passed on for centuries to each and every young woman that my daughter, nieces and nephews, grandchildren and great-grandchildren will someday be blessed to have. I truly hope this book becomes a keepsake for them to share.

I want to thank my nephews, Justin and Brandon, and my niece, Brooke, for helping me accumulate some of Bess's insight through the years. I love you all and am so proud of the adults you have become. I also want to thank my brother Bud and his wife Robin who've shown what it is like to truly care for a parent, working as a team to support Mom's wishes to remain independent for as long as possible in a house and home she truly loves. As well, I want to thank her many aides, especially "Lu Lu", whose gifts of caring and compassion are beautiful every day.

I want to thank my very special girlfriends: Kerry, my longest friend from childhood who befriended me as a newcomer to the area when I was 14; Laurie, my little sister from my college sorority who is in all aspects the little sister I never had; and Wanda, my friend I met when our daughters were in kindergarten who has the unique gift of making each and every person she encounters feel truly special. Each of these women came into my life at pivotal times and encouraged me to push myself to new levels. Each of them brings a unique perspective from their own life experiences which have been invaluable for me. I love you all, my family and friends, beyond words.

About the Author

Bonnie Lorber Habyan is an author, speaker and chief marketing officer working in real estate finance. Before getting her MBA in banking and finance, Habyan was a corporate spokesperson, news reporter, radio DJ for a call-in love songs program and Miss Baltimore Oriole—the latter of which led to meeting her husband John Habyan, an MLB player with whom she just celebrated her 30-year wedding anniversary. She is also a mom to her amazing daughter Holly, who is in law school. Habyan and her family just moved to South Carolina after living in New York for 25 years. *The World According to Bess* is her first book.

Made in the USA
Columbia, SC
11 October 2022

69282894R00102